WHY CAN'T WE TRUST GOD?

WHY CAN'T WE TRUST GOD?

FOUR SORROWS THAT LEAD US TO TRUST

Thomas Wise

Zion Press

Zion Press
1601 Mt. Rushmore Rd, STE 3288
Rapid City, SD 57702

Ordering Information:
Quantity sales. Special discounts are available on quantity purchases by corporations, associations, and others. For details, contact the "Special Sales Department" at the address above.

Why Can't We Trust God?/Wise —1st ed.

ISBN 978-1-63357-189-1

Library of Congress Control Number: 2019944289

First edition: 10 9 8 7 6 5 4 3 2 1

What Others Are Saying

Why Can't We Trust God? is recommended reading for Christian adult believers and thinkers, and focuses on the latest scientific evidence supporting belief and the Word of God. Tom P. Wise's purpose and focus is clearly presented in introductory paragraphs that combine science, news, and affairs of belief and the heart:

> In this book we are going to explore what it means to trust in Jesus, and to trust in our God––who is the Father, the Son, and the Holy Spirit. As we broach this subject, we will dig into concepts of suffering as they are presented in the Bible and in issues of trust as they are described in current academic research. Combining the two elements of academia and faith may provide for us a picture by which we may choose to trust in Jesus, God's only son.

This blend of perspectives from both scientific and faith-based examinations allows readers to contemplate not just the meaning of God's Word and Biblical promises, but the scientific evidence that support them. Additionally, Wise creates a blueprint for this progressive examination and follows it religiously: "As we progress through this discussion, we will learn together how the three bases of trust form our ability to choose to trust. These bases are personality, cognition, and institutional trust."

Chapters stick to Wise's plan as they document God's consistency in his message, advocating a form of attention and listening which encourages not only introspection and belief, but cultivating time to truly listen and perceive this message in daily life:

> God does not need us in order to carry out his plans. He provides us with opportunities to participate in his plans so that we are blessed by doing his work, and that others can see God in us and in our lives. By listening carefully, God will tell us what he is doing and then we can do his will.

One doesn't anticipate an injection of autobiography into such a treatise, but Wise adds observations of life that includes his own, juxtaposing Biblical passages and quotes with his own experiences to pinpoint moments of enlightenment and realization. This creates a multifaceted, human approach to spiritual understanding that encourages his readers to adopt their own reflective process from a combination of reasoned examination and Biblical study, daily life experiences, and scientific knowledge.

The result is a survey recommended for any thinking Christian who would better understand the nature of God's actions in the world, the process of both watching and acting, and how to link personal objectives and goals with God-driven belief.

Christians will find *Why Can't We Trust God* empowering, enlightening, and rooted in personal, political, religious and scientific experience.

—D. Donovan, Senior Reviewer, *Midwest Book Review*

Why Can't We Trust God? by Thomas P. Wise is a book that gives us a blueprint of how to lead a life of service to God through trust and suffering. Wise tells us that there are three bases of trust that form our ability to choose to trust -- personality, cognition, and institutional trust. He posits there are four sorrows we face in life, Life in a Fallen World, Pain Due to our Sin, God's Pruning, and the Hate of the World, all designed to point us to God. Using scripture and modern-day science and thinking, Wise deftly intertwines the two to show us a path that brings us closer to God and what he wants us to do in service to him. Wise shows us how we develop trust in our lives and how that trust can lead us to salvation through Jesus Christ, and then how that trust can lead us to a fruitful life of service to God. Wise goes through the four sorrows one by one, showing how pain and suffering have all been designed to impact our lives and to lead us to Jesus and a closer walk with Him.

I thoroughly enjoyed this book. It really made me think. Using scientific reasoning along with scripture really opened my mind to Adam and Eve in the Garden of Eden, and what that really represented for mankind. Always using scripture to back his teaching, and throwing in personal experiences that show how suffering affected his life deepened the message Wise presented. I would really recommend this book to those who are seeking Christ and for those who have accepted Him and are looking for a way to serve God by having a closer walk with Him.

—Richard L. DeMoss, *Reader's Favorite*

To my children, grandchildren, nieces and nephews, and, of course, my parents, that they may have a close, trusting, and loving relationship with Jesus. And, to my wonderful wife of thirty years this year, Nancy; I love you.

Trust in the LORD *with all your heart and lean not on your own understanding; in all your ways submit to him, and he will make your paths straight.*

Proverbs 3:5-6

Contents

List of Tables

Love the Lord Your God

Hear, O Israel: The Lord our God is one
Lord: And thou shalt love the Lord thy God
with all thine heart, and with all thy soul, and
with all thy might. (Deuteronomy 6:4-5 KJV)

66 "Trust in the LORD with all your heart and lean not on your own understanding; in all your ways submit to him, and he will make your paths straight" (Prov. 3:5-6 NIV). For years and even today, I sit in my living room each day and watch the news, reeling as the wheels seem to have come off this crazy world of ours. For a while there, every time I tuned in to one of the 24-hour news channels, anchors expounded upon the devastation of Christians in the Middle East. Heads were removed, families burned alive, and children crucified for refusing to denounce their trust in Jesus.

News casts displayed the ravaging of entire generations of Christians, and the vanishing of whole communities in the mayhem. In Iran and Turkey, the Christian has almost disappeared (Griswold 2015). The number of believers in Iraq is less than half of what it was in the 1970s, dropping from 4% of the population to less than 1% (Tristam 2017). In other nations, including Egypt, home of the largest Christian population in the Middle East, churches are regularly attacked and destroyed, and female Christians are forced into sexual slavery. In Egypt, one's religious affiliation is stated on the State ID (Sherwood 2018). Unfortunately, Egypt's state ID makes it easier to identify and persecute Christians. And yet, Christians in the Middle East hold fast to their trust in God.

We don't suffer the same persecution as our brothers and sisters in the Middle East. In the United States, we enjoy the freedom to worship according to our own conscience. Yes, some believers do suffer abuse in the courts and are devastated financially and emotionally by a legal system that is drifting from the roots of the constitution. And these faithful believers, too, hold steadfast to their faith.

It is hard to watch the news and even harder to explain God's love to friends, coworkers, and family members as they too suffer through another news day of mayhem and pain. And yet, we know that God is good, that he loves us and cherishes our love for him. Suffering is, and for some populations always has been and remains, a way of life, and yet the passion these people show for Jesus is unwavering.

In this book we are going to explore what it means to trust in Jesus, and to trust in our God––who is the Father, the Son, and the Holy Spirit. As we broach this subject, we will dig into concepts of suffering as they are presented in the Bible and into issues of trust as they are described in current academic research. Combining the two elements of academia and faith may provide a picture by which we may choose to trust in Jesus, God's only son.

God, in his unwavering love for us, developed his story over several thousand years. In God's own unchanging and all-knowing way, he painted for us a cohesive, concise, and accurate picture of life on this Earth. Through his Word, God illustrates an experience that he knew would be painful, but ultimately rewarding: one that, through suffering, would point us toward him.". God's Word tells us of Four Sorrows we face in life, which, through perseverance, we will overcome. These Four Sorrows are Life in a Fallen World, Pain Due to Our Sin, God's Pruning, and the Hate of the World––directed toward us when we live for Jesus. All are designed to point us toward God.

We live in a fallen world. Life on Earth is tainted by the sin of God's children. This truth is the beginning point of pain and suffering, and ultimately the beginning of our understanding of God's love and faithfulness. Through illness, aging, and our own mortality, we learn of God's unwavering desire for a relationship with us so that we may know him better.

In our desire for self-fulfillment and sin, we build walls between God and ourselves, behind which we hide and cower while knowing that God still sees us. Sin separates us from God's love. Yet we can, and do, learn about ourselves and our need and ability to turn to Jesus with hope. Before Jesus, each of us possesses a personality hampered by our sin, but one that may strengthen our resolve to trust through grace.

Jesus, who is our mediator, stood before God in our place to take the punishment for our sins. As we come closer to God and his Son, we become his. And as his, God's own child, we suffer under God's loving hand––just as a child suffers when they are spanked and sent to their room to think about what they did. Jesus says God prunes the branches, forcing growth and the production of healthy fruit. Pruning hurts but is ultimately good for the vine. Through the process of pruning, we learn about God's grace and love, and come to understand that God is trustworthy.

Ultimately, we are God's children through our acceptance and love for his Son, Jesus. But, as we draw closer to Jesus and choose to trust in him, the world turns against us. Jesus told us that the world will hate those who choose to love him––and hate hurts.

As we progress through this discussion, we will learn how the three foundations of trust form our ability to choose to trust. These principles are personality-based, cognitive-based and institutional-based trust. We can then understand how to trust our

Lord Jesus for mediation and forgiveness, God's Holy Spirit for guidance, and God the Father for redemption and eternal grace.

Acknowledgments

I want to thank my dear wife Nancy for her support, and Peter McSain, my brother in Christ, for reading and providing feedback.

CHAPTER 1

The Sorrow of a Fallen World: Where Our Personality Is Formed

*Then the Lord God formed a man from the
dust of the ground and breathed into his
nostrils the breath of life, and the man became
a living being.* (Genesis 2:7)

God's Word goes on to describe how man was formed. God created a garden called Eden into which he placed the man, whom he called Adam. Then Adam walked with God as the first witness to God's creation, enjoying the freshness and comfort of walking among God's creation (Isaiah 43:10, NKJV). Living in fellowship with his creator according to God's design, Adam wandered along the river banks and through all kinds of trees and shrubs that were both good to eat and pleasing to the eye. God charged him with caring for the garden. God created all people that we may glorify him and that we may fellowship with Jesus, his Son (Isa. 43:7, 1 Cor. 1:9).

The newly formed man walked through the garden daily, talking with his Father. God tells us Adam and Eve "heard the sound of the Lord God approaching" (Gen. 3:8 NKJV). God strolled with Adam among his creation, and they formed a relationship.

Does this passage mean that God physically walked in the Garden of Eden with Adam? Did Adam know God in human form? Since Adam and Eve both believed that they could hide from God, it is logical to assume that God must have manifested himself to them in a form that was finite in appearance.

Many scholars argue that no man has ever seen God face-to-face, for to see God's face is to die. The writer of Exodus 33:22 explains that God protected Moses from God's glory, telling him, "When my glory passes by, I will put you in a cleft in the rock and cover you with my hand until I have passed by" (NIV). So how, then, could Adam survive living in close proximity with God, let alone take walks with God in the garden? We must remember that Adam was created for eternity. He was created free of sin, holy and righteous in God's eyes. Adam was created in God's image: holy, eternal, never changing, merciful, gracious, long-suffering, abundant in goodness and truth, forgiving transgression and sin—to name only a few of the attributes of Adam's creator.

Therefore, being made in the image of God, Adam, created into eternity and free from sin, is righteous, possessing the attributes of his creator and able to stand before God. For if Adam was not created holy, then he was created without hope, trapped in an eternal existence, for death had not entered into the world. He would therefore be flawed, eternally banned from the presence of God, and the fall to sin would have no meaning. Further, if Adam was created not in holiness and able to be in the presence of God, then he was created lower than we who are born into sin.

For to have sin is to be separated from God. Adam was therefore eternally separated from God if he was not holy at creation, lacking the hope we possess of death and resurrection into the presence of God. We are created with hope, for as the apostle Paul said in 2 Corinthians 5:8, "We are confident, yes, well pleased rather to be absent from the body and to be present with the Lord" (NKJV). John, the disciple whom Jesus loved, said, "[We] shall see His face..." (Rev. 22:4 NKJV).

The next time we hear of God walking among men is with Jacob––and in the New Testament as Jesus walked, taught, and lived among the people of Israel. Later in history, the Israelites never expressed any thought of hiding from God, for God appeared to them in a cloud during the day and a pillar of fire at night. God watched over them, reflecting his power and protection, but did not walk among them.

Now we know that our God is a triune God. God formed Adam saying, "Let us make mankind in our image, in our likeness" (Gen. 1:26-27). God expresses himself in three persons––God the Father, God the Son, and God the Holy Spirit. Or perhaps we can better understand the three persons of God in another way; God's Will, God's expression of his Will, and God's Spirit which enables us to accept and follow his Will. Matthew explains for us, that, "Out of the abundance of the heart the mouth speaks" (Mat 12:34, NKJV). The Will has expression only in words or deeds, thus out of the abundance of God's heart he provided his expression through his son, Jesus.

We know this because God tells us that, "In the beginning was the Word, and the Word was with God, and the Word was God" (John 1:1). God spoke the world into being. Psalm 33:9 tells us that "he spoke, and it came to be." God brought the world into being through his Word. John goes on to tell us that "through him all things were made; without him nothing was made that has been made." He also said, "The Word became flesh and made his dwelling among us" (John 1:3; John 1:14). We know, therefore, that Jesus is the physical, creative, and personal form of God that interacts with his creation. That is not to say that in the Garden of Eden Jesus was in human form, for to be in human form is to be born into this world by a women or to be a created being, but it does appear that he was in some physical form when he dwelled with Adam in the garden.

There are other preincarnate examples of Jesus taking the form of a man. Genesis 32:24-30 states that Jacob "wrestled with him till daybreak." When the man was unable to overpower Jacob, he touched Jacob's hip and caused it to dislocate. In the form of a man, the Lord did not, through physical force, overcome Jacob, but supernaturally dislocated his hip with a touch. At the time of the encounter, Jacob did not know that he wrestled with the Lord. As with the disciples who walked with Jesus along the road following the resurrection thousands of years after Jacob's encounter (Luke 24:13-35), Jesus allowed Jacob to understand who he was before departing. The man told Jacob, "Your name will no longer be Jacob, but Israel, because you have struggled with God" (Gen. 32:28).

Now, we must always remember and understand that God never changes. The author of Numbers challenged our understanding of God in saying, "God is not human that he should lie, not a human being that he should change his mind. Does he speak and then not act? Does he promise, and not fulfill?" (Num. 23:19). God does what he says and says what he does. He does not promise, and then choose to do otherwise. Jesus Christ, who is God's only begotten Son, does not change, the writer of Hebrews tells us (Heb. 13:8). And James 1:17 says God, "who does not change," is the giver of every good and perfect gift, while Ephesians 4:8 tells us Jesus is the giver of gifts.

Therefore, since John recorded Jesus's words when he said, "I am the way and the truth and the life. No one comes to the Father except through me" (John 14:6), we can believe that Jesus is the Word. And the Word is God, likely interacting with Adam in the form of a preincarnate man. Genesis 3:8 states that Adam and Eve heard the Lord walking. It is my conjecture—and thus only an opinion—that Adam physically walked through the garden with the Lord Jesus. This is important because the personality of a human develops as they interact and model the behavior of significant people in their lives. Adam strolled among Jesus's creation, exploring the world as a new being, learning to behave in a way pleasing to God——and, like all human children, forming a personality through which he would filter all of his experiences.

What does personality have to do with trust?

Modern psychologists tend to lean toward the idea that one's personality is developed in the early stages of life, and contrary to previous thought on the subject, continues to develop as one matures over the years. However, generally speaking, the basis of our personality is pretty well established by around the age of 7, about 10% of our expected lifespan (Live Science Staff, 2010). Therefore, since he lived to be 930 years old (Gen. 5:5), Adam's personality was likely well established by age 90.

It is difficult to know Adam's physical age upon creation. This continues to be a point of discussion among, perhaps not scholars, so let's just say interested parties. If we run a simple search of the Internet, we find thousands of entries discussing the age of Adam at the point of creation. There does not appear to be any consensus regarding Adam's physical age when he is created, or how old Adam may be when he made the fateful decision to disobey. We can assume by Adam's behavior that he was likely old enough to procreate and old enough to choose to make his own decision rather than to obey, but not old enough to take responsibility for his choices. This description implies that Adam was very probably between the ages of 13 and 20 in physical and emotional maturity.

This is the most likely age since when God created Adam, God told him to, "Work it and keep it" (Gen. 2:15). God's charge to Adam required that he have the physical stature to perform the work. God also blessed Adam and Eve "and said unto them, be fruitful, and multiply, and replenish the Earth, and subdue it" (Gen. 1:28 KJV). Therefore, Adam and Eve must have both been created at an age at which they would have the emotional and physical maturity to have a sexual relationship––which, according to Huberman (2016), puts their likely age range at a minimum between 13 and 17.

From an emotional perspective, children will learn to accept responsibility for their actions during the developmental years of 12 to 19 (Bastable 2003). So, Adam was old enough to manage the garden and to procreate but he did not immediately accept responsibility for his decision to participate in eating the forbidden fruit, so it is unlikely that he was out of his adolescence at the time of the fall. Now, is this conjecture? Absolutely, for we have no accurate means by which to measure his age at creation, because the Bible doesn't reveal this information. So, therefore we can project that Adam was likely created between the ages of 13 and 19 physically, and had likely not reached age 20 when he was driven from the garden. His personality was still developing, and he endured a tragic developmental experience.

Our personalities are based on the experiences in our lives. We learn to define what we may trust by the result of the actions of those close to us. As children, we learn early in life that our hunger is satisfied by our caregiver. Thus, we trust that the one who loves us is the one who feeds us. Adam learned that God is holy and just. God can always be trusted to do what he says he will do, and to care for us and stand by us even when we fail. Our parents' response to our requests for food, warmth, comfort, and protection builds our trust in them. The personality traits they display become part of our definition of trust.

Unlike in Adam's world, comprised soley of the Garden of Eden, our lives include other children. Our lives include school, with teachers as role models, and peers who are very eager to help us understand what trustworthiness means. Classmates are always more than willing to help define what may be trusted and what should be concerning:

"Jimmy is a liar."

"Joey takes stuff that aren't his."

"Sally called me a bad word."

And so, by our parent's response to our unwanted behaviors and how that response makes us feel, we learn what actions cannot be trusted. By the time we hit third grade, our understanding of trust is well grounded in experience. We grow through our school years and discover that some behaviors remain consistently good and others consistently bad. We learn that some acts are threatening and can be trusted to hurt us, whereas other practices are good and can be trusted to please us. Consistency provides a rubric by which we measure potential outcomes and thus add to our definition of what is trustworthy.

Although no child likes it, by middle school we began to figure out that our parents were usually right in telling us to stay away from certain kids, not go to certain places, and not try certain things. We learned that we could trust that bullies were always mean, even when they would try to be nice. They just couldn't help themselves. In the end, the bully could always be trusted to be the bully. Thus, for most of us, when a friend's behavior became inconsistent, it was far more confusing than when a bully tried to be a friend.

Our desire for consistency, and for people to fit within our definition of trustworthiness, determines our friendships––even when those friendships may be damaging to our wellbeing. But how do we develop an understanding of trustworthiness when there is no lack of trust? What happens when every need is met? It is likely safe to say that we have all met that child whose every need is met. It is easy to identify the child who has never waited to be fed or was never told "No" when expressing a desire. This is the child who will scream in the grocery store until they receive the cookie, or drop to the floor in the toy aisle, thrashing and wailing––until the mom or dad gives in and agrees to purchase that coveted item. For this child, share means my turn, not yours, and hunger demands immediate satisfaction. I'm not talking about the little one who's parent walked the child from store to store for hours on end, before the child finally gave in to exhaustion and lashed out. I'm talking about the kid who is fresh and complains with enthusiasm until they get what they want. I'm talking about the entitled one, the child that believes they can, and will, get what they want if they stick with it and keep on screaming.

Now imagine a relationship with a Father where we have no choice but to accept all things freely and without reservation or failure, as with Adam. All of his needs were met by God. Adam lived in paradise, where food was abundant and days were always sunny—with a cool fresh breeze, lush lands, trees for shade and fruit, and our Lord Jesus at his side. It never rained. Instead, the ground was provided moisture through a mist, and the Earth responded to Adam's effort with fresh vegetables daily. His crops never failed due to pestilence, disease, or lack of water. He never experienced fear or illness, and never knew hunger or the meaning of work.

God knew what Adam needed before he asked, although I am sure Jesus allowed Adam time to ask. As we noted earlier, God never changes. So, as he does today, he provides the opportunity for us to ask for what we need before he responds with an answer to our prayer. Still, we receive so much more than for what we request. And so, the question must be raised concerning our ability to love a Father when there is no choice but to love: do we love that Father when we have no alternative by which to measure our love?

According to Smith, love is a choice that we make, whether for our spouse, our children, our parents, or our God. If love is a feeling, then we can fall in and out of love, but if we choose to express love, then we can choose to continue to love. "It is a choice to see good in our partner," or in any other being (Smith 2018). Yet again, how can we choose to love someone if we do not know there is an alternative?

Love and trust are linked. It is because love begins with a relationship, an understanding on each other's desires and mutual interest—plus a comprehension of one another's physical needs and personality. God wants an intimate sharing of desires, interests, needs, and personality flaws and strengths with us, and through this relationship, love. We have all heard someone say the words, "I fell in love." Maybe we've said it once or twice ourselves, or used the phrase, "I've fallen out of love"—as if love is a perilous stroll along the edge of a cliff. Isn't it great that God chooses to love us rather than relying upon a fleeting feeling?

Feelings change and are unreliable. Our bodies are designed to sense different experiences of our world. We can feel the warmth of the sun on our skin and the chill of the early morning breeze on our face. When we touch a hot pot on the stove, we recoil involuntarily to prevent serious injury. But the sensation of touch is not reliable. Cold, when too intense, is translated as a burn in our minds. Our minds, while wonderfully crafted by God, are intentionally limited.

Jesus said, "You did not choose me, but I chose you" (John 15:16). The words of Jesus are a comfort, because we have confidence that Jesus chose us. Our God chooses to love us and therefore his love will never change. God will not fall out of love with us even when we have not chosen him. God is consistent, never changing, and therefore committed to his choice to love.

Adam and Eve's choice in the garden destroyed the connection we once had to God's creation and creative genius. We once knew God face-to-face, but "for now we see through a glass, darkly" (1 Cor. 13:12 KJV). As Paul wrote to the church in Corinth, we perceive the wonder of God's creation and the universe through a diseased and battered lens. Due to the corruption of the fall and the limitations of our comprehension, we often experience opposites in the same way, through a muddled lens of understanding.

According to Barrett (2017), our minds attempt to articulate what we experienced in the past to simulate what we experience today as a response to new sensory inputs. Our brain gathers input from our senses and makes a best guess of what to expect based on previous patterns (Barrett, 2017). Barrett goes on to explain that, thinking, perceiving, dreaming, and emotions are believed to use the same mental process (2017). Feelings of love, hate, fear, and power can elicit the same emotional response: tears. Emotions have a way of stressing our bodies. Both good and bad emotions affect us in the same way, and the intensity of the effect is compounded by its duration. As stress builds up, chemicals in our bodies are released, triggering the endocrine system to release hormones—activating the tearing response, allowing the flow of moisture to flush these chemicals. We shed tears of happiness and hatred, fear, and attraction. Tears don't distinguish between emotions.

Connor says scientists discovered that the same nervous circuits in our brain that set off the feeling of hate also trigger the feeling of love. The hate circuit shares some things in common with the love circuit: "Love and hate are intimately linked within the human brain." Perhaps, Connor contemplates, this may explain why both hate and love "will result in similar acts of extreme behavior" (Connor 2008).

Fear and attraction affect us in the same way. These emotions trigger the same fight or flight reaction. Intense attraction often causes us to repel the suitor much the same way that we attempt to drive off an attacker. This is best observed in young people when they first begin to notice the opposite gender. Remember the experience of trying to ask a girl to your first high school dance? Your heart raced, your palms got sweaty, and your mouth went dry as you approached. Then you quickly turned away, pretending to see something extremely interesting down the hall, while she looked at you with that scrunchy-eyed, puckered expression, puzzled by the sudden swerve as you tried to avoid her gaze. We rebel against love in the same way we protect against an attack. Our emotions are utterly unreliable. Love is complete, or may be described as fulfilling when it is first experienced through understanding, as a friendship in a trusted relationship.

We cannot love, Gettel (2003) tells us, until we can truly trust. We can only experience a deep bond if we can trust–that is, if we can allow ourselves to be vulnerable, take a risk, develop real relationships, and love. Scientists in the twenty-first century have taken many hours of painstaking research to understand the mechanics of trust.

Boteach (2011) argues that love requires hate and that we have no love because we have forgotten how to hate evil acts of aggression and devastation. Humanity in the twenty-first century has become desensitized to acts of evil (Bugeja 2017). Users will tune into all forms of social media to watch as victims are beaten or tortured, and millions sit fixated as terrorists torture and mutilate. We don't hate bombings of innocent people and attacks by evil governments against Israel. When we practice love without hate, we lack the will to stop evil acts against the faithful.

The writer of Proverbs 6:16-19 tells us, "There are six things the Lord hates, seven that are detestable to him: haughty eyes, a lying tongue, hands that shed innocent blood, a heart that devises wicked schemes, feet that are quick to rush into evil, a false witness who pours out lies and a person who stirs up conflict in the community." We know that God hates sin. Psalm 5:4 says that God is not a God who takes pleasure in wickedness. God is holy and therefore there is no sin in him. Hamada (2016) describes holiness as the complete absence of sin. And in being holy, only God may define sin and save us from sin (Hamada, 2016). Jesus tells us that a house divided against itself cannot stand, and thus sin cannot exist in God's presence, for God never changes, always was and always will be and therefore cannot fail (Matthew 12:25).

Adam and his helper Eve, who lived in God's presence in the Garden of Eden, never having experienced pain or hate and having had all things provided by God who loved them, having never experienced anything other than love and the care provided by God. They did not have any choice to make beyond accepting God's provision and love. So, the question becomes, did they know they loved God, or did they merely feel loved? For years, Adam lived in God's presence and had not yet experienced anything else.

The Fall and Curse

By allowing a serpent to tempt Adam to misbehave, God allowed a situation in which Adam had an alternative. For the first time, Adam was able to choose to behave and follow God's command, or to rebel and follow his inclination to explore alternatives. In accepting the option to taste the one fruit in the garden from which he was forbidden to eat, Adam's choice resulted in a new normal––although tragic beyond his understanding—in which he might discover his love of God.

We must always remember that God does not need to discover our love for him. God is omniscient and knows our heart. As the writer of Proverbs tells us, "A person may think their own ways are right, but the Lord weighs the heart" (Prov. 21:2). The author of Samuel tells us that we, as fallible beings, look at a person's outward behaviors and hear their words, but God looks at our heart (1 Sam. 16:7).

Our heart is the seat in which spiritual connections, emotional desires, and wisdom come together in our decision making. It is the part of us that drives our choices and determines whether we choose to abide in God or choose the physical world. You see, Adam always had a choice, but he never acted upon that alternative. It was not until a friend or peer, or in this case—and even worse yet—someone whom he was to lead, poked at a nerve, making Adam feel small by pointing out that he had a choice.

Eve did respond to the serpent explaining that she was allowed to eat from every tree, but not the one in the center of the garden. The tree in the center was likely just another tree. God told Adam and Eve not to eat fruit from this tree because it held the knowledge of good and evil. It is my contention that this tree, in holding the knowledge of good and evil, was no different than the other trees. What this tree represented was the choice to obey or disobey. It is because God held nothing in all the world from Adam and Eve. Not a plant, or animal, or tree, or any other living or non-living thing in all of God's creation was held back from their desire or need, except for one tree in the center of the garden.

It is like owning the largest toy store in the world and allowing your children to have anything they want, except for one toy that sits in the center of the store like a crown jewel on display. And your children enter the store and choose anything they want, and it is given to them. Each time they enter the store, they are going to go straight to the center and gaze upon that toy before reluctantly turning away and finding something else—something inferior to that one toy.

Eventually, your children are going to turn to you and say, "I want that toy."

Your answer, of course, is always the same: "No, dear. I love you, but you cannot have this one. You can have any other toy in the store you want, but this toy is special. This toy is different, and if you play with it, you're going to die."

So, they go off again and find another toy. At some point the children are going to think to themselves that this toy looks exactly like the other toys. It's made of plastic, seemingly the same plastic as all the other toys. Then, as they stand there gazing at the toy, the cool kid from down the block walks over. He sees your kids walk in every day and take anything they want because

Dad owns the toy store. Today, frustrated by seeing your children get anything they want, he decides he wants to see your children get in trouble for taking the special toy.

I can imagine the way the exchange between Adam and Eve went down:

Serpent: "Did God really say, 'You must not eat from any tree in the garden'?" (Gen. 3:1).

He stretched out the words, trying to bait Eve into an argument.

Knowing the crafty animal should not be in the garden at all, Adam took a step toward the serpent, then stopped and watched, wondering how Eve was going to answer the question.

Eve: "We may eat the fruit of the trees of the garden; but of the fruit of the tree which is in the midst of the garden, God has said, 'You shall not eat it, nor shall you touch it, lest you die'" (Gen. 3:2-3 NKJV).

Adam: "Hey, yo, don't," he said raking out the dirt around the base, losing interest in the subject and turning back to work. "God said don't. Eve, you know—"

Adam allowed the serpent to cut him off, not really paying attention. Before the morning mist started, he wanted to get the central flowerbed fluffed, and slowly turned the soil.

Serpent: "You will not surely die. For God knows that in the day you eat of it your eyes will be opened, and you will be like God, knowing good and evil" (Gen. 3:4-5 NKJV).

He smiled, tilting his head slightly to appear more innocent as he told what he knew to be a half truth, realizing half a truth is still a whole lie.

Adam: "Don't listen to him," He said somewhat apathetically as he continued with his work. He watched the exchange out of the corner of his eye, wondering. Adam stopped, straightened, mouth agape, and stared silently as the serpent leaned back against the Tree of Knowledge of Good and Evil that stood tall and strong alongside the Tree of Life.

Serpent: For emphasis, he crossed his arms as he scratched his back against the one tree that God said you shall not eat, or so much as touch, or you will die—and smiled as Eve's eyes widened with surprise. He raised his eyebrows and held out one hand toward a piece of fruit, palm up as if serving it to Eve.

Adam: Adam watched in silence, waiting to see what would happen next. *Tell her no*, he thought to himself. He started to reach toward Eve, then froze as the serpent looked at him with eyes that accused him of being a coward. Adam's eyes hardened and narrowed, staring back.

Eve: Eve tilted her head and contemplated the serpent. *He's still alive,* she reasoned, then looked up at the fruit to which the serpent gestured. "So when the woman saw that the tree was good for food, that it was pleasant to the eyes, and a tree desirable to make one wise, she took of its fruit and ate" (Gen. 3:6 NKJV).

Adam: *Coward*, Adam said to himself. He was close enough, and he thought, *Slap her hand. She knows better. You do too*, he said silently to himself, watching. Eve handed a piece of the fruit to him, then took a big bite of her own as Adam waited to see what would happen. He pushed out his lower lip ever so slightly and looked at her eyes. She's fine, he thought, taking a bite of his own.

Was it peer pressure that made Adam fail? Adam made a choice to experience more of the physical world than was allotted to him by God, thus separating himself from God's will in his life. The serpent was "being more cunning than any beast of the field" (Gen 3:1 NKJV). This meant the serpent was cleverer than any of the other animals in Eden, twisting God's words, knowing that God was talking about an eternal existence that would not be possible if we chose to live outside of his will. For sin, which is an act of disobedience and therefore rebellion, cannot exist in God's presence. God is holy and just, never changing or wavering from what is right. Thus, sin separates us from God and must be corrected.

It is the same with our own children. In order for a child to grow to be a person capable of living in harmony with our world, the child must learn to behave in ways acceptable to society. It is the same in God's presence in Heaven. We need to learn to live in harmony with God's presence in Heaven and are therefore required to learn God's way: love.

It wasn't about the fruit at all. The fruit doesn't represent sex like some commentators believe, nor does it represent lust, or coveting, or anything so deep and theological. The issue at hand with Adam and Eve was the simple point that they always had a choice to make. God provided them the ability to choose to obey God's will, or to turn away and choose their own direction. The fruit in the center of the garden was a choice, and at the point when they chose to eat that one special fruit in the center of the garden, they chose their own path.

The tree at the center of the garden represented Good and Evil. Good was the choice to remain in God's will. Evil was the choice to follow their own path, stepping outside of God's will and therefore choosing to sin. Adam discovered that he had many choices in life. He could choose to serve God or serve himself—and when this realization became clear, he felt naked, exposed, and unclean. He became ashamed of his choice and hid from God.

Due to Adam's choice, our world is cursed. The curse, while it hurts and causes us pain, sweat, and blood, is designed to ensure we can come to understand God's love for us. God's curse reminds us of the choice Adam made and the consequences of sin. God takes care in the words he uses.

The Serpent

The serpent must have held a high place among the animals in the garden, for Eve trusted him to the point where the two of them apparently had an ongoing relationship. The Bible does not record that the serpent introduced himself and spent time convincing her to listen. There is no back and forth as the serpent tried to break down her defenses, causing her to believe that she should choose his side over God's command not to touch the tree. Stewart (2018), an online blogger with interest in the fall of Adam and Eve, asks the question, how the serpent came to be in the garden? Did the serpent sneak in with the purpose of deceiving God's children? Why does he speak at all? For many, the answer to both questions is that the serpent must be a symbolic representation.

In Numbers 22:21-39, the story of Balaam and his donkey shows us that if God chooses, animals can speak plainly to us. But if the relationship doesn't exist before the animal takes a lead role in the event, it does take time for the person to believe the animal. Balaam beat his donkey for stopping and refusing his commands until God opened Balaam's eyes to see what the donkey was trying to tell him. But in Genesis, Eve simply accepts what the serpent has to say. So, we can gather that Adam and Eve both knew the serpent from past experiences, thus assuming the serpent to be trustworthy.

The serpent lost his place of honor and the close relationship he enjoyed with man. He was made to crawl in the dirt among those who once were his peers. And until Jesus returns in the end days when the curse is lifted, the serpent is pitted against mankind. Serpents no longer enjoyed a close and friendly relationship with people. We also know that God is just and punishes the sin of the individual, not the sick or those indwelled by demons.

In this case, unlike all other cases of demonic possession, the serpent is directly accused and punished by God. "And the Lord God said unto the serpent, Because thou hast done this, thou art cursed above all cattle, and above every beast of the field; upon thy belly shalt thou go, and dust shalt thou eat all the days of thy life: And I will put enmity between thee and the woman, and between thy seed and her seed; it shall bruise thy head, and thou shalt bruise his heel" (Gen. 3:14-15 KJV).

Likewise, Jesus never mistook demon possession for illness or as a choice to sin, but instead, he recognized the demons and spoke directly to them. When Judas Iscariot betrayed Jesus, God made it clear to us what happened.

> And the chief priests and the scribes sought how they might kill Him, for they feared the people. Then Satan entered Judas, surnamed Iscariot, who was numbered among the twelve. So, he went his way and conferred with the chief priests and captains, how he might betray Him to them. (Luke 22:2-4 NKJV)

And in the case of the men who lived in a cave along the road, Jesus accused the demons of their actions, and not the demon-possessed person. Matthew wrote:

> When he arrived at the other side in the region of the Gadarenes, two demon-possessed men coming from the tombs met him. They were so violent that no one could pass that way. "What do you want with us, Son of God?" they shouted. "Have you come here to torture us before the appointed time?"

> Some distance from them a large herd of pigs was feeding. The demons begged Jesus, "If you drive us out, send us into the herd of pigs."

He said to them, "Go!" So, they came out and went into the pigs, and the whole herd rushed down the steep bank into the lake and died in the water. Those tending the pigs ran off, went into the town and reported all this, including what had happened to the demon-possessed men. Then the whole town went out to meet Jesus. And when they saw him, they pleaded with him to leave their region. (Matt. 8:28-34)

The men, now freed from the demons, were not punished for their crimes of violence, but rather freed from possession and allowed to go without condemnation. And in the example of Luke 4:33-35, Jesus freed a man from an unclean spirit while teaching in the synagogue. Again, this man was not punished or accused. And, as a final point in this discussion, I would suggest that Mary Magdalene, a woman freed from the indwelling of seven demons and the one to discover Jesus's resurrection from the dead, is honored as the person to wash Jesus's feet with her hair and a jar of alabaster (Luke 7:37; Luke 8:2). Mary Magdalene is mentioned seven times in the Bible due to her close relationship with and devotion to Jesus, but is never accused or punished for her behavior.

So, it follows that God, who is just, only punishes the sinner to provide for the forgiveness of the sin. Lucifer is never mentioned in the story of the Garden, for this is not the case of his rebellion, but rather of the serpent's rebellion against God, perhaps trying to elevate himself. I propose that the serpent was condemned because, while influenced by Lucifer to do an evil thing, it was not possessed. The serpent made a choice to plot with Lucifer to mislead Adam. Remember that God's own words describe the serpent as the most clever of all the animals in the garden. And, since God is just, the sinner is directly held accountable for their own sins. The serpent is punished, as are future generations who will feel the effect of that punishment, although they do not carry any guilt due to the serpent's lie in the garden. Future generations are a testament to the original sin and God's consistent holy and just act.

The Woman

The woman is reminded of the pain God experienced when his children rebelled against his will at the onset of childbirth: "I will make your pains in childbearing very severe; with painful labor you will give birth to children" (Gen. 3:16). We know of the pain and real dangers of childbirth, but did you realize that the pain has a purpose in reminding us how God suffered when his children chose to reject his will for their lives? God watched as his children were condemned to an eternity of separation from him. He could no longer enjoy long walks in the garden as he taught them to love one another and his creation. As with the serpent, God is holy and just, and sin carries consequences (though not condemnation) that are often felt for generations.

God also condemned women to desire their husband, but what does that really mean? The apostle Paul explains this to us in writing, "But I would have you know, that the head of every man is Christ; and the head of the woman is the man; and the head of Christ is God" (1 Cor. 11:3 KJV). Paul continues to explain as he writes to the people of Ephesus, saying, "For the husband is the head of the wife, even as Christ is the head of the church: and he is the savior of the body" (Eph. 5:23 KJV). Therefore, in addition to her pain in childbirth, the woman's curse was to be removed one step from her previous relationship with God. But also, the curse is a picture of the need to desire God above all things.

The effect of the consequence of our sins is felt for many years. This is most easily seen in the sin of adultery. Families are often torn apart and re-formed many times with children and parents mixing to form new families, creating complex relationships with multiple layers of pain and suffering that affect generations. Many times, trust is so severely damaged that people will turn away from God and teach their children and grandchildren to flee from the church. The effects of sexual sin strike deep into our souls and cause us to continue to sin, further damaging our relationship with God, and eroding the trust of future generations.

But God is just and holy, and continues to pursue us to be sure that our children and our children's children will return. He continues to make a way home, for he hates the sin, but loves the sinner. We, and our children, feel the effects of the original sin, but God is true, holding open the door so that we can know he is trustworthy and full of love for us.

The Man's Curse

Adam did not escape the situation unscathed. Men are cursed for not performing the duties assigned to Adam in the Garden of Eden. Adam was charged as caretaker for the garden and was to be the boss over all living creatures. He was given the task of naming all things and leading them in God's will, but he failed. The act of naming has a specific meaning in many cultures. To name something, according to *Culture Decanted*, an online blog (www.culturedecanted.com), is an act of acknowledging and claiming power over the thing named. Therefore, God told Adam to consciously claim his power over all of God's dominion and recognize his responsibility. God wants us to know that we are his, for he revealed in Isaiah 49:1 that he knew our names even before we were born.

The serpent was not corrected by Adam, as a good leader would do, but instead the snake was allowed to take a leading position, pulling others off the proper path of life. With Eve, Adam did not correct her incorrect thinking, but rather allowed her to lead him astray.

Because Adam did not fulfill his role in the garden, the ground was cursed, causing it to no longer volunteer sustenance, but rather to harden and harbor weeds and thorns. Mankind now toils in blood, sweat, and tears as we struggle to pull nourishment from what was once a bountiful and enjoyable harvest. God says, "By the sweat of your brow you will eat your food until you return to the ground" (Genesis 3:19). The beauty of the curse is the need to continuously toil over what was once an easy life, causing mankind to remember God's desire that we are to care for and properly manage the resources he provides.

God did not intend that we should live in a state of decline or disobedience to him, therefore he declared that "since from [the earth] you were taken; for dust you are and to dust you will return" (Gen. 3:19). Thus, death, as God first told Adam, is the result of willful disobedience. Suffering in this life reminds us that Adam once lived freely and without suffering, enjoying the fruits and foods provided by God in the garden. But in God's amazing grace, death is not the end of the story, but rather a path forward in our journey back to relationship with him.

God Wants a Relationship with Us

God wants a relationship with us, but he wants us to choose to love him, and that choice was not possible until we had an alternative. In allowing us to decide between himself and a want to satisfy our own desires, we may learn who we love more God or ourselves. However, we are forced to encounter a picture of what separation from God is like when God allows us to make a choice between his will and our own, and it hurts.

God said, "I am the vine; you are the branches. Whoever abides in me and I in him, bears much fruit, for apart from me you can do nothing" (John 15:5 ESV). Now, God does not choose words without care. He uses the word *abide*, which means to bear patiently and to wait, remaining in a fixed state (Merriam-Webster

May 24 2019). We must bear the trials and sorrows of this world with patience, remaining with and connected to the Lord, hearing his voice and following his lead as we wait for this curse to end according to God's plan. The curse has an expiration date, but as Jesus told us, not even he knows the day (Matt. 24:36).

So, in other words, God wishes to be close to us, sharing in our pain and suffering, trials, and difficulties as we are fed, comforted, clothed, and as we receive provisions from the Lord. God wants a relationship with us. To choose, we must have the chance to select between two or more alternatives to determine which of the posed opportunities is best. Thus, while God did not create Adam's sin, he did choose not to prevent the possibility of sin.

Our personality is formed in this fallen world. In our early years, unlike Adam, we encounter a conflicting series of messages from parents, caregivers, peers, and siblings––plus random encounters with other relatives and strangers. These encounters inform our definition of what it means to be trustworthy. For many people—those raised in a faithful and consistent Christian home—the definition lines up well with a belief that Jesus loves us and has only our good in mind.

Perhaps your definition of trustworthiness was founded on the security of work and money. For others, *trustworthy* may mean anger, violence, abusive language—or perhaps a danger far less aggressive or obvious such as ambivalence, a lack of passion, or apathy. God does not want us to be lukewarm about him. He wants us to make a choice to love and accept him: "I know your works: you are neither hot nor cold. Would that you were either cold or hot! So, because you are lukewarm, and neither cold or hot, I will spit you out of my mouth" (Rev. 3:15-16 ESV).

You know what lukewarm is like. Imagine picking up a cup of your favorite hot beverage after it has sat too long, waiting for you to return and finish drinking. You raise it with anticipation of that creamy heat and take a cautious slurp, and you get a tepid slap in the face. You grimace as if in pain and quickly dribble the liquid back into the cup with a moan. *Yuck.*

Remember the heart palpitations, butterflies in your stomach, and gnawing anticipation that you can't wait 'til Friday. Your first deep and real love? Remember how your arms ached to hold them close at the end of a long week, finally able to see them again? Oh, how you groaned at every stop light, "Come on, come on," you urged the old man driving in front of you, ten miles under the speed limit, and you pleaded with every traffic signal as you approached, "Please stay green." You finally get there and are just about step out of the car before it comes to a complete stop. Then you practically float to the door of the apartment building, and she rings you through the entrance. And you take the stairs two at a time, finally arriving. The door opens, and with a smile that won't quit, you enter. You embrace and say those three words: "I love you." But the love of your life once again says nothing.

The object of your love is deeply in *like* with you. Oh, how you hate that. That is the pain God feels when he says he loves you. Oh how painful it must be when the object of God's love remains deeply in like with him. John wrote that, "We love him, because he first loved us" (1 John 4:19 KJV). We need to realize that the curse under which this world struggles is not because God wants to punish us, but rather so that we can come to understand that we have a choice between going our own way or choosing a God who loves us, and whose arms ache to hold us close.

Science accepts that our personality can continue to form based on current experiences (Bryner 2007). Thus, when we shake off a definition of trust that is contrary to God's personality of love, honesty, integrity, consistency, holiness, and justice, we can discover a world in which pain and sorrow are balanced with God's joy. God has given us an opportunity to have a love much greater and deeper than the one into which Adam was born. We were born into a world with suffering and sorrow that will continuously point us back to him in a way that provides a feeling of great happiness in times when sorrow is overwhelming.

CHAPTER 2

The Sorrow of Personal Sin: Where Our Personality Meets God

The four living creatures, each having six
wings, were full of eyes around and within.
And they do not rest day or night, saying:
"Holy, holy, holy, Lord God Almighty, Who was
and is and is to come!" (Rev. 4:8 NKJV)

Just as was Adam banished from God's presence in the Garden of Eden when he chose to disobey, so our sin also separates us from God. Sin cannot exist in the presence of a holy and just God. So Adam was thrust from the Garden of Eden and guards were placed at the entrance of the garden to prevent him from returning (Gen. 3:24). But we must first ask, what does it mean when we say that sin cannot exist in the presence of God? The answer to this question is complicated, so bear with me as we explore this question.

We were created as eternal beings in God's image as body, soul, and spirit. Our soul is the image of the Father, the eternal part of humanity that lives on and animates our human self. The spirit is the conscience, the helper that guides our decisions and leads us in accordance of God's will. As we are told in 1 John 4

(NKJV), there is more than one spirit, and therefore we must take care that it is the Holy Spirit in us. For the Holy Spirit does dwell in those that accept the Lord as their personal savior (1 Timothy 1:14). And finally, we have our body, our human form, as Jesus is God in human form.

Sin, as we established earlier, separates us from God's will. His spirit lives within his faithful children, and therefore we know that sin does not drive God from us. We do know that, as the apostle Paul wrote to the church in Rome, "the wages of sin is death, but the gift of God is eternal life through Jesus Christ our Lord" (Rom. 6:23 KJV). So, we know that when we sin, we are separated from God, who offers us eternal life. We see this separation in Jesus's death upon the cross. He died with the sin of all mankind heaped upon him as the final judgment of our sin. The sun went dark all over the world as God turned his face away from our sin and Jesus cried out, "My God, my God, why have you forsaken me?" (Mark 15:33).

We know that God is holy because Isaiah told us, "For so says the high and lofty One who inhabits eternity; whose name is Holy; I dwell in the high and holy place, even with the contrite and humble spirit, to revive the spirit of the humble, and to revive the heart of the contrite ones" (Isa. 57:15 NKJV). So, since God is holy in all forms, and the place where he dwells is holy, then sin prevents us from dwelling in eternal places and following where God leads. To be holy means to be set apart from defilement, or, said differently, to be set apart from that which may cause us to seek things other than God's will.

Peter describes God's desire for us to be holy when he records Jesus's words, saying, "You must be holy, because I am holy" (1 Pet. 1:16 NLT).Paul continues this explanation, telling us, "to offer your bodies as a living sacrifice, holy and pleasing to God- this is your true and proper worship" (Rom. 12:1 NIV). Butwhat does it mean to be a living sacrifice?

The word *sacrifice* is defined by Merriam-Webster (May 24 2019, Definition of Sacrifice) as to suffer loss, give up, renounce, injure, or destroy, especially for a belief, or end. In a letter to the believers in Rome, Paul explained that, "The wages of sin is death" (Rom. 6:23 KJV). Because sin is rebellion against the King, death is the only just punishment, but God made a way for us to avoid the consequence. In the Old Testament, the people of Israel were commanded to assent to a series of blood sacrifices to atone for, or cover over our sin. Therefore, if we are to be a living sacrifice, Paul is conveying to us the need to suffer loss or destruction of our worldly desires in order that we may draw closer to God––and be made holy by him, set aside for him and his service.

Paul is not the first to talk about being made a living sacrifice for God. In the book of Judges, we meet Samson. Samson was a man born to Manoah, a man of Zorah whose wife was barren and so unable to bear children. God came to Manoah's wife and told her she was to bear a child who would be a Nazarite, set aside for God's purpose to deliver God's children out of bondage. Samson was to be a living sacrifice to God to atone for the Israelites (Judg. 13).

Conformed to Christ, an online blog (www.conformedtochrist. org 2011), summarizes the commands upon Samson as he is set aside for God's purpose as the following:

- For a specified period of time.
- Refrain from consuming any part of the fruit of the vine or from using anything made from grapes.
- Do not cut the hair of their head during the time of the vow.
- Do not touch a dead body, not even the body of a close relative who might die during the time of the vow.
- When the time of the vow was completed, specific offerings were to be brought to the Lord, and the person was to

shave his or her head and place the hair in the fire under the sacrificial offering.

So, as Paul described for us the need to be a living sacrifice to God, he expressed a biblical concept that would have been familiar to the people of Israel, but not clearly understood by his gentile followers. He is telling his followers to stand out in this world as different from everyone else, transform their minds to conform to the life for which Jesus died, that they may be holy. Paul tells us to set aside our desire for power, money, strength, beauty, or whatever consumes our hopes, and instead to desire the holiness that God offers.

God Gives us a Picture of Human Holiness in His Commands.
God's commands and the picture of holiness in this life were given to Moses in the form that we remember as the Ten Commandments.

> I am the Lord your God, who brought you out of Egypt, out of the land of slavery.
>
> You shall have no other gods before me.
>
> You shall not make for yourself an image in the form of anything in heaven above or on the earth beneath or in the waters below. You shall not bow down to them or worship them; for I, the Lord your God, am a jealous God, punishing the children for the sin of the parents to the third and fourth generation of those who hate me, but showing love to a thousand generations of those who love me and keep my commandments.

You shall not misuse the name of the Lord your God, for the Lord will not hold anyone guiltless who misuses his name.

Remember the Sabbath day by keeping it holy. Six days you shall labor and do all your work, but the seventh day is a sabbath to the Lord your God. On it you shall not do any work, neither you, nor your son or daughter, nor your male or female servant, nor your animals, nor any foreigner residing in your towns. For in six days the Lord made the heavens and the earth, the sea, and all that is in them, but he rested on the seventh day. Therefore, the Lord blessed the Sabbath day and made it holy.

Honor your father and your mother, so that you may live long in the land the Lord your God is giving you.

You shall not murder.

You shall not commit adultery.

You shall not steal.

You shall not give false testimony against your neighbor.

You shall not covet your neighbor's house. You shall not covet your neighbor's wife, or his male or female servant, his ox or donkey, or anything that belongs to your neighbor. (Exod. 20:2-17)

To follow God's commands is to abide in him and to be holy. Yet, God knew no man would ever be able to choose him in all things. We have too many opportunities every day to choose God or to pick our own way, and in almost every case we decide to please ourselves instead of our Maker and King. Oh, I am not talking about big things like murder. Most of us will never attempt murder or hold up a bank. Or will we?

Have you ever fantasized about something to the point that you startled yourself with the vividness of the daydream? I'm not talking about the fleeting dreams we all have—the zoning out during the day when we get bored type of daydreaming. Have you ever loitered on a thought, conjuring up the feelings behind the event and the desire to follow through, lingering over the details? Perhaps you were able to visualize the day, smelled the freshly mown grass where you planned the event, and heard the cries of your victim when you got even?

I know this sounds dramatic, but many of us have had these thoughts after a particularly traumatic betrayal. I'm sure many people who were mercilessly bullied in school went through the exercise many times over in their heads as they found a way to get even. It is only human to lash out at the people who hurt us. I have dreamed many times about building a "007 car" of my own, complete with razor cables I could drop the next time I am tailgated. In my head, I watched as the cable dropped and the impatient driver behind me popped their tires and fell away. In my head, it was real.

Fantasy is an abandonment of what is. It is not being present in your today, but rather living in a time in the past or one possible future (Brown 2012). God, through his thoughts and words, spoke and all that is seen and unseen came into existence. God simply said, "Let there be light," and light existed. The mind of God makes all things exist. And we are created in God's image. Now, I'm not trying to say that we, mere mortals, can think things into existence with the exercise of physical actions—but our minds do create a reality that we often find hard to separate from our physical reality.

Our minds have the ability to feel pain in a limb that is no longer part of the body. According to Lewis (2013), leftover representations in the brain of an amputee are behind the phenomenon of phantom limb pain. The brain, it seems, creates the sensation of pain due to the expectation of pain (Mayo Clinic 2018). People have also experienced feelings that the limb still exists and senses cold or tickling. Our mind creates the reality that we experience.

According to Schnider (2008), our brain is so powerful that it can create an entire past in our lives that never existed. While the experience of feeling and seeing things that don't really exist is most often associated with a diseased state, the effect is the brain creating a new reality. Jesus does recognize the impact that our fantasy life can have on our relationships with others and with God. While explaining God's commandment not to commit adultery, Jesus went one step further, "But I tell you that anyone who looks at a woman lustfully has already committed adultery with her in his heart" (Matt. 5:28).

Jesus knows that our mind will pull us away from abiding in him, which is why Paul wrote to the church in Corinth, admonishing them to take every thought captive to keep their minds obedient to Jesus (2 Cor. 10:5). The writer of Proverbs told us that as we think in our heart, the basis of our feelings, so we are (Prov. 23:7). In other words, our thoughts tell us about our heart. This means we have an opportunity to do something about our relationship with God before we dwell on things that are not pleasing to him.

In his blog *Active Christianity* (www.activechristianity.org 2018), Lenk explains to us that God's Word is our weapon against our own thoughts. When we keep God's Word in our heart and call it to our attention when our thoughts tempt us, we can remain in abidance with God. Just as Jesus did when tempted to turn rocks into bread, we must call upon the Word of God to drive these thoughts back into captivity.

As we noted earlier, to choose our own way, even if only in our thoughts, is to choose sin and therefore death. So, rather than requiring our own death to pay for our sin, God created a system of animal sacrifice as a temporary covering of our debt as payment. Through this continuous sacrifice, our sins were covered over, but not removed, and our holiness was renewed. Under the old system of forgiveness, sin required a continuous payment of blood , so God provided a temporary surrogate for us. Today we know Jesus as that surrogate, our Savior, but we will get to that later.

The commandments of God are like the bumpers placed in the gutter at a bowling alley that guide the ball toward the goal at the end of its journey. When the bumpers are in place, we may send the ball rolling with confidence, knowing that no matter how poorly we propel it forth, it will hit the mark. In the same way, these commandments form a path by which we may walk toward God throughout our lives. However, we can, if we choose, manage to overrun the bumpers and end up in another lane, free to crash into the gutter and miss the mark entirely.

In this analogy, the bowling ball is our decisions as we navigate through life, the bumper is God's commandment, and the rebound is our reaction to sin when we discover the consequence. God has placed the fenders in the gutter so that we may know his will. When we are small, we will always stay within God's will, rebounding and learning more about God's plan every time we turn away from sin. We ricochet down the lane, learning our place within God's commands. But, as we grow, our own will becomes stronger, until we can jump those bumpers and end up in a completely different lane—or worse, choose to switch lanes altogether. In our analogy, there are many lanes available, but only one with God's commandments to guide our path.

Matthew recorded Jesus's words, telling us, "Enter by the narrow gate; for wide is the gate and broad is the way that leads to destruction, and there are many who go in by it. Because narrow is the gate and difficult is the way which leads to life, and there are few who find it" (Matt. 7:13-14 NNKJ). We have the entire bowling alley of life available to us. God's words, in the form of the Ten Commandments given to Moses and recorded in Exodus, give us the path as originally described by God to guide us toward home. And, although God provided a means of cleansing and renewing in the form of the animal sacrifice to cover over our sins, he knew that his children would wander and be unable to follow the path.

God sent his son, Jesus, as the final sacrifice, freeing us from the bondage of the continuous cycle of sin and payment. We are released from the debt for our sin from which we could never escape in this life—an existence in which every activity and every decision was a continual decision to follow God, or make our own path. As Jesus hung on the cross, paying that final sacrifice to cover over the sin of mankind, he said, "'It is finished!' And bowing His head, He gave up His spirit" (John 19:30).

That never-ending cycle of sin and sacrifice was broken by Jesus's obedience to the Father, being the perfect and final sacrifice. The path home, while still narrow, was now made safe for us to walk—making the best decisions we are able as we attempt to follow Jesus down the path, bouncing from bumper to bumper in the bowling alley of life. But what does this all mean? It means that God, in the original decision faced by Adam, created a world for all mankind that is self-correcting.

Our world and the way we interact within it is designed to point us back to God. When we make a decision that is contrary to the commandments that God laid down for us, we separate ourselves from God's will. In so doing, we encounter pain in the form of punishment, and often in the way of the consequence for our action. Paul recorded Jesus's words when he said, "Let every soul be subject to the governing authorities. For there is no authority except from God, and the authorities that exist are appointed by God" (Rom. 13:1 NKJV).

So, God created the governments throughout the world as a means of correction. Through correction, we are able to identify when we wander from the path. Now, the challenge here is knowing that not all government is God-centered, and not all lawmakers will abide by God's will. Remember that we live in a fallen world, beset by sin and separation—a world that is controlled by evil, for in the curse this world was given over to Satan (Job 9:24). But again, in giving this world over to evil, a way was created to guide us back toward God in all things, negotiating our path by process of discomfort and correction.

That is not to say that if we live for God and follow his path explicitly that we will not suffer pain, but that pain has a different purpose that we will explore later. Then how do we follow God's path if every encounter requires a decision? Our definition of trustworthiness needs to be adjusted so that we trust in God to guide us. Jesus told us, "Truly I tell you, anyone who will not receive the Kingdom of God like a little child will never enter it" (Mark 13:15).

Without hesitation, children trust anyone that loves them first. *The Parent Tool Kit* (www.parenttoolkit.com 2018), an online blog, states that we begin to establish a child's sense of trust as early as infancy when we respond to the child's physical and emotional needs. When discomfort comes to an infant in the form of wetness, cold, hunger, or heat, the child expresses their need by wailing. No matter the time of day or night, the child will call out. When that call is heeded, the child registers the caregiver's response in their memory. The caregiver's response is then measured against the next response, and the next. And with consistency in meeting the child's needs, thus reinforcing the attachment the child feels. the caregiver begins to create a picture for the child of what is trustworthy.

The child senses your love through your ability to meet the child's most basic needs. That love, according to Gutierrez (2013), develops into trust and affects the formation of the child's brain. This helps the child to feel secure and enables the child to handle stress later in life. For those of us who have ever had the privilege of caring for one of God's gifts to the world, know that a little one will not hesitate to take that leap of faith.

When my children were small, they would climb up on the couch, or some other high place. A huge smile would form on their faces as they leaned over the edge and launched themselves toward me, knowing they would never hit the ground. No matter what happened, they knew that I would catch them, breaking their fall as they landed securely within my arms. They never feared, for they had no doubt of or care for their own well-being as long as their trusted parent was nearby.

My children felt safe as they leapt into the deep end of the pool because they were sure they would never sink as long as I was there. They would climb anything and simply let go because of their trust in me. As they grew and chose to explore their abilities, they were willing to try bicycling, skateboarding, skiing, and so on, because they believed they were safe. When authority figures in a child's life set forth rules and follow through consistently in their behavior, the child's sense of what is trustworthy is further developed and reinforced.

With consistency, that bond of trust can become unshakable. We still belong to a fishing and beach club in the Midwest where my wife and I once lived. We would take the children swimming all summer long, whenever the weather allowed. Here, our children learned to swim. Even now they can swim for what seems like hours without any need to touch the bottom. We tease our oldest daughter, telling her she floats like a bobber. She just won't sink. But, when she was around the age of three, she didn't swim very well yet, so she just liked to walk in the water. One day, while we focused too much attention on the youngest one while teaching her to swim, the older daughter decided to step out a little deeper.

She trusted us completely, believing we were smart enough to never lead her into a perilous situation, even by accident. She walked until the water was over her head, and then, staring up at us while holding her breath, waited calmly for someone to lift her out of the water so she could once again breathe freely. She stood there smiling, waiting to be saved because she was near the ones whom she trusted without fail.

A child with a strong bond, an unshakable sense of trust, will not hesitate to turn and run toward the voice of the mother or father. As adults, Jesus wants us to act in the same way as an adult. He wants us to know his voice and therefore trust in him, running toward him when we hear him. John recorded Jesus saying, "My sheep hear My voice, and I know them, and they follow Me. And I give them eternal life, and they shall never perish; neither shall anyone snatch them out of My hand" (John 10:27-28 NKJV). He guides us down the path in a way that will allow us to navigate this world and avoid the bumpers, rolling toward the goal with as little pain as this fallen world will allow.

How Do We Regain That Kind of Childlike Trust?

Science tells us that we need a place that we call home for trust to develop: a place where we have membership with others of the group. I'm not talking about sitting in the same pew or chair during the same hourly service each week in the same church building that your family has attended for the past thirty years, or perhaps even thirty generations. No, I'm talking about a place where you can be you, with all of your warts and bruises along with everyone else's flaws in full view. Membership means that people know you and you aren't able to hide anything. That Home-Feeling comes from a place where you walk in and someone yells, "Tom is here," and you feel like you landed in a safe place where your burdens fall away; where the weight of the day is shed like an old coat in a warm room. Membership is a place where you know the processes, rules, norms, roles, and names. And I'm not only talking about a place where everyone knows your name.

A Home-Feeling comes in the presence of the people who love us as we are, in a place where our needs are met like those of a small child. For most of us, we grew up in a home where we cried and someone fed us without having to ask. When our diaper was wet, someone noticed, and it was changed out for a fresh, clean, dry diaper. We never had to lift a finger to make it happen. This was a place where the child never had to be brave or pretend to be someone they were not. All warts and defects were openly displayed, and we were loved regardless. That is home.

Home is best found in the presence of believers with a healthy and robust home fellowship program, where believers regularly welcome each other home. These are the people who watch for you and recognize you no matter where you are. They spot you in the grocery store and welcome you with a smile and a hug, and they call you when they haven't seen you for a couple of days. Your home fellowship group is consistent, loving, and never judging. They are open and honest, and consistently apply the commandments that God gave us thousands of years ago. When any one of them wanders off and hits a virtual bumper, the rest are there and ready to provide guidance and support.

It is in this place that we can see God modeled for us in a consistent and safe way, allowing us to see trustworthy behavior in the way that God intended us to see it. We need the model set plainly in our sight every day to overcome the flawed image of trustworthiness that is developed in a fallen world. In this place, we can expose our heart to our home fellowship family and invest our time and treasure in support of our brothers and sisters with confidence.

Why do we need to adjust our paradigm of trust when our parents met our needs, setting the example of consistent behavior, in our early infancy? Because we also saw the cartoons on Saturday morning filled with violence that never really killed anyone but was acceptable for solving any problem. We saw that our siblings could take our things, but never really get caught, and that our friends could cheat on the test and still get a good grade. As we grow, we figure out that breaking the rules and misbehaving is acceptable—even expected in certain circles. Our heart becomes tainted by this realization and our picture of *trustworthiness* changes shape, the edges becoming blurred.

"Blessed are the pure in heart, for they shall see God," Matthew recorded Jesus as saying (Matt. 5:8 ESV). And Luke, in his research, continued the sermon: "For where your treasure is, there will your heart be also" (Luke 12:34 ESV). What does this mean? God is telling us to love and trust as a child loves and trusts, without reservation and in totality, believing that he in whom we trust can be invested with all of our heart. We can know that he accounted for every need.

According to a study of the use of the word in the bible conducted by Dr. John Uebersax, the heart, is a place where our personality, our being, is expressed—a place where our cognitive and personality-related perception is filtered and integrated with thought and purpose. Uebersax concludes that the heart is at *the core or center of the person* (Uebersax 2012). Writing in the *Bibles for America* blog (http://blog.biblesforamerica.org/what-is-the-heart-in-the-bible/2015), one author noted that the heart is the integration or expression of our soul and spirit, the place where we love.

Personality-based trust is built upon the relationship skills our parents taught us early in life, but often that training is flawed, impacted by our parents' fears and biases. As young children, we build a framework of what, to each of us, trustworthiness means. Trustworthiness, openness, and a willingness to reciprocate—as well as some aspects of our attitude toward risk—are traits that each seeker brings to the church and are the foundation upon which we can build closer relationships. It is up to each one of us—elders, deacons, the church management team, and members of the congregation—to create an environment that supports personality-based trust.

How can we, as churchgoers, build such an environment? Won't churchgoers and new seekers naturally sort this level of trust out for themselves? The answer is both yes and no. We might simply assume that a person's natural instinct to build relationships will take care of this problem without the need for any active participation by leaders. Bonds will form, but this process does not happen well on its own, nor should it be merely an accidental operation.

> "The King will reply, 'Truly I tell you, whatever you did for one of the least of these brothers and sisters of mine, you did for me.'

> "Then he will say to those on his left, 'Depart from me, you who are cursed, into the eternal fire prepared for the devil and his angels. For I was hungry and you gave me nothing to eat, I was thirsty and you gave me nothing to drink, I was a stranger and you did not invite me in, I needed clothes and you did not clothe me, I was sick and in prison and you did not look after me.'

> "They also will answer, 'Lord, when did we see you hungry or thirsty or a stranger or needing clothes or sick or in prison, and did not help you?'

"He will reply, 'Truly I tell you, whatever you did not do for one of the least of these, you did not do for me'" (Matthew 25:40-43).

So, what does this mean to us as we seek to realign our model of trustworthiness? As we join with other believers, building strong and healthy relationships based on transparency and mutual support, we learn to reevaluate what trustworthy means. We discover that our parent's model of manhood, womanhood, and parenthood was fatally flawed. A strong man is not always one that never cries, can fire a weapon spot-on at three hundred yards, never feels pain, remains forever silent and stoic, ferociously protective of country and family. These are excellent traits for a United States Marine and, these are fine traits for a protective father when his daughter begins dating (believe me), but won't always work when seeking to understand God.

We must be vulnerable and honest, willing to be mutually dependent with both strangers and loved ones. Americans are fiercely independent and traditionally ambitious, willing to sacrifice family and friends to fulfill the American model of success. We forget—or perhaps never realized—that through dependence and transparency we draw closer to the model of trust and relationship that God seeks for us.

Therefore, "seek first the kingdom of God and His righteousness, and all these things shall be added to you" (Matt. 6:33 NKJV).

CHAPTER 3

The Sorrow of God's Pruning: Where We Decide to Serve God

I am the true vine, and my Father is the gardener. He cuts off every branch in me that bears no fruit, while every branch that does bear fruit he prunes so that it will be even more fruitful. (John 15:1-2)

As the Father has loved me, so have I loved you. Now remain in my love. If you keep my commands, you will remain in my love, just as I have kept my Father's commands and remain in his love. (John 15:9-10)

You are my friends if you do what I command. I no longer call you servants, because a servant does not know his master's business. Instead, I have called you friends, for everything that I learned from my Father I have made known to you. You did not choose me, but I chose you and appointed you so that you might go and bear fruit—fruit that will last—and so that

> *whatever you ask in my name the Father will*
> *give you. This is my command: Love each other.*
> John 15:14-17)

God, Jesus explained to the Sadducees, is the God of the living, not the dead. He is the God of Abraham, Isaac, and Jacob, who live, having been transported to Heaven for eternal life. They live as we too will live if only we trust in Jesus, the only Son of the living God. Hearing that Jesus had silenced the Sadducees, the Pharisees got together. One of them, an expert in the law, tested him with this question: "Teacher, which is the greatest commandment in the Law?"

Jesus answered the Pharisee, the expert in the Law, telling everyone who would listen, "Love the Lord your God with all your heart and with all your soul and with all your mind. This is the first and greatest commandment" (Matt. 22:37). Jesus then added, "And the second is like it." He told them to, "Love your neighbor as yourself" (Matt. 22:39).

Riley, an expert therapist writing for the Christian Broadcasting Network, described our ability to love—to live in a trusted, connected relationship with one another—as a bond of trust. Breaking this trust, according to Riley, is like losing your heart—one broken piece, or relationship, at a time (Riley 2017).

What we experience in the early years of our lives lays down layers forming our heart like sediment, filtering our hurts, hangups, and fears into who we become. As we develop and our view of the world begins to emerge, the word trust takes on meaning, evolving into our personal expression of trustworthiness. Through the repetition of met expectations, we learn to assume that these hopes will continue to be fulfilled. We tend to build our own belief system as to how the world around us works, creating a sense of equity or fairness.

Each layer provides the basis on which we trust one another, the institutions with which we interact, and of course, our God.

We bring our model of trustworthiness, and an expectation for how those around us may behave in relation to that model, into every situation. We also develop an intuitive ability to measure and ascribe trust in and to each other—and to assess how well we measure up to others in regard to how fairly we are treated. Researchers at Washington State University described the layers of trust as *personality-based trust, institutional-based trust, and cognitive-based trust* (Sarker, Valacich, Sarker 2003).

When God first called us to him, he revealed himself through other believers—perhaps in the form of a song we heard on the radio or through a loved one who insisted we follow them to a church service. We filtered this information through our model of trustworthiness, testing everything by our definition of what a trusted relationship looks like. God may not fit that model, but our friend did. Or perhaps the words to that song struck a painful memory that caused us to listen just a little closer that day.

As our relationship with God grows, our thoughts, fears, desires, and pain are exposed as God reveals more of himself to us through our reading and interaction with other believers. In the Bible, we discover a group of early adopters called disciples. Through their actions and interactions with Jesus, we find our own shortcomings revealed. In learning about them, we see that our own faults are already known to God.

A relationship requires reciprocation. This means that as God reveals himself to us, we must reciprocate and expose more of ourselves to God, thus closing the loop and building a closer understanding of each other. God desires relationships, not just cognitive knowledge of his existence. However, before the relationship can develop, that cognitive learning must take place.

So, God built a model in his Word, the Holy Bible, through Jesus's interactions and reciprocation with his disciples. God gave us this book so that we may learn about our history and about his character as he interacts with and guides his people, Israel, into a relationship with him. It is God's wish that, through coming to understand him and his people through their stories in his Word, we will learn to trust in his Son Jesus. In business, this is called "swift trust": an acceptance of a trusted relationship developed over time by previous group members that is adopted by new group members (Jarvenpaa & Leidner 1998). New group members assume trust to be valid based on the interaction and learning of previous members, allowing time for their own trust to be validated and developed through their own experiences.

So, how does God develop a means by which we may assume he can be trusted? He does so by revealing himself in the Old Testament writings, through his consistent and fulfilled promises to the people of Israel, and through Jesus to the disciples. In doing so, he reveals our own shortcomings to ourselves, and shows us that he loves us despite our flaws. The disciples were not eloquent, learned, influential, righteous, drawn from high society, or respected in the synagogue. As table 1 shows, they were people just like us: flawed, scarred, and scared.

Name	Occupation	Description	Flaws
Andrew	Fisherman	Businessman	- Ran when Jesus was arrested.
Peter	Fisherman	Businessman	- Impulsive - Prone to boasting - Violent - Scared and denied Jesus 3 times

James	Fisherman	Businessman	- Loud (brother of thunder) - Mother peeti-tioned Jesus for favor - Ran when Jesus was arrested
John	Fisherman	Businessman	- Loud (brother of thunder) - Mother peti-tioned Jesus for favor - Ran when Jesus was arrested
Matthew (Levi)	Tax Collector	Government Employee	- Cheating - Over-charging - Sided with the enemy - Ran when Jesus was arrested
Simon	Zealot	Anarchist	- Ran when Jesus was arrested
Judas	Thief	Embezzler	- Stealing - Turned on Jesus
Philip	Unknown		- Ran when Jesus was arrested
Thomas	Unknown		- Required physi-cal proof of Jesus - Ran when Jesus was arrested
Thaddaeus	Unknown		- Had little to say - Ran when Jesus was arrested

James (sof of Alphaeus)	Unknown		- Ran when Jesus was arrested
Paul	Pharisee		- Murder - Legalism

Table 1. The Flaws of Jesus's Disciples

When we continue reading, taking a close look at the great men of God as revealed to us in the Bible, we see that the list of flaws gets very long, so I am only going to list a few (see table 2). So why does God show us the weaknesses of his faithful? So that we have a mirror in which to see ourselves and better understand our relationship with God––because the beginning of a healthy relationship is the sharing of our self with others.

Name	Occupation	Description	Flaws
King Saul	King of Israel	Farmer, anointed King by Samuel	- Attempted murder _ Sought guidance from witch.
King David	King of Israel	Farmer, anointed King by Samuel	- Adulterer - Murderer - Ate bread from altar - Naked in public
Samson	Judge	Dedicated to God at birth	- Gave away his secret for a girl

Moses	Prophet	Saved at birth, Prince of Egypt	- Murderer - Bad temper
Elisha	Prophet		- Murderer (killed with bears) - Bad temper
Solomon	King of Israel	Wisest and richest man ever to live	- Depression - Tried all earthly pleasures

Table 2. Flaws of the Great Men of the Bible

"Throughout history, God has always used the least likely and the most unqualified to provoke change. The Bible is full of misfits—those who usually lost out on man's approval but always won with a God-dreamed vision" (Schatzline 2015). God does not use the righteous and the powerful to do his work; rather he employs the misfits and miscreants. God chose "the foolish things of the world to shame the wise; God chose the weak things of the world to shame the strong, and in so doing shows us his faith and love" (1 Cor. 1:27).

When Paul prayed for healing of his weaknesses and physical ailments, God said to him, "My grace is sufficient for you, for my power is made perfect in weakness" (2 Cor. 12:9). . "Therefore," Paul declared, "I will boast all the more gladly about my weaknesses, so that Christ's power may rest on me" (2 Cor. 12:9). God wants us to know that he loves us and that we can come to him as we are. He loves us in all of our weaknesses and flaws so that we have the strength to release our fears, allowing to come to him and open up about our own shortcomings. By revealing ourselves to God, we become vulnerable and are able to learn more about him.

Before we can build a strong, healthy relationship with God, Jesus who is God's Son, and the Holy Spirit of God, we must be able to discover who God is and allow him to strengthen the bond he has with us. Remember, relationships begin with discovery. And discovery allows for the development of cognitive-based trust—That is, a trust built on evidence that someone is trustworthy. This includes our stereotypical perception of someone. While stereotypes tend to have poor connotation, and often are used to reinforce poor expectations of people or groups, good stereotypes are often formed around our expectations of biblical personalities. A belief that biblical characters are bigger than life and more worthy of God's love than are we can make us feel small and incapable of being loved by God.

To some degree, almost every person and group is influenced by a learned stereotype of what constitutes a biblical personality. I thought that the disciples were faith-filled, upstanding models of what a Christian should be, growing continuously in the image of Jesus and harnessing the power of the Holy Spirit in every interaction with the mere mortals with whom they interacted. I believed that people like King David and the prophets were undoubtedly clear images of God on Earth—especially since David was called a man after God's own heart (Acts 13:22).

But when I took the time to read and learn, I discovered something about God: God loves and uses flawed people. God uses our weaknesses to help us grow in our knowledge of him when we allow him to work in our lives—and when we accept the offer to participate in what God is doing. He uses our flaws so that people may see God at work in our lives. Before we get into the topic of participating in what God is doing, let's explore a better understanding of cognitive-based trust.

Cognitive-Based Trust

When we were young, we learned to watch out for the bully by watching someone be bullied or experiencing bullying ourselves. We quickly figured out that aggressive behaviors were often displayed by people who enjoyed making others feel bad. Bullies hurt someone just for the fun of it, or to make themselves feel more powerful and in control. We learned who our friends really were in a pinch by experiencing their support when we were bullied—maybe they were the only one present when we experienced some sort of trauma or event.

Even small events like forgetting our homework taught us something about our friends. Was a friend always driven by integrity and therefore not willing to give up the answers to our homework when we forgot our own? This taught us that this was a person of integrity that could be counted on to guide us. I often discovered that kids like this were churchgoing kids. I didn't know what that meant at the time, but I always knew that the kids who went to certain churches were different than the rest of us.

As our learning expands, "it creates an understanding of the world around us. Cognitive trust is a trust that we choose to place in a person, group, or program based on information that we have gleaned from our past" (Wise 2013). As we apply our past learning to similar situations, we may decide if trust is a reasonable response to the conditions we face. According to Mizrachi, Drori, & Anspach, writing in 2007, the learning is often enhanced if we have a solid belief that we may have a future relationship with the individual or group.

So, if we have a good experience and we expect to have contact with that person or group in the future, the expected continued relationship can strengthen our current level of trust. This is because when we assume that a trusted condition or relationship will remain, it will cause our reliance upon that condition or relationship to grow. What does that mean? It means good expectations can lead to more good experiences.

As a kid, I played a lot of sports. Growing up in a military family in the US, the expectation was that all the guys played organized baseball, football, and basketball, depending on the time of the year. Often one of the dads coached the team. On the first day of practice we would all gather at the field. The first to arrive watched as each of the kids showed up. One at a time, each team member would emerge from the car with a parent and then join those already present to watch for the rest of the team, waiting to see who would approach carrying a rucksack filled with sports equipment. As the designated dad-coach showed himself, we would keep a close eye, watching for some clue about how to build our expectations for the season.

As the dad-coach emerged, the discussion would immediately begin. Questions flew around the team gathered on the field. Someone would ask, "Anyone been on his team?" We would either hear enthusiastic responses from those with good past experiences, or groans and warnings from those with bad past experiences.

The first set of inputs in everyone's decision to trust or not to trust was the past experiences offered by anyone with something to share. Team members would share stories from friends and past teammates about the coach's style and reputation for fairness. We would all keep an eye on the coach to see who had joined the entourage as he emerged from the car. Once again, groans and moans or excitement and anticipation would pass among the crowd based on the company that the coach kept. The reputation of those accompanying the coach would have an immediate effect, either positive or negative, in our decisions to trust in our coach. If the coach's kid was a solid athlete and had a reputation for hard work and fair play, that too would color the thoughts of the players as they gathered information regarding the new coach.

The next input was the first words from the coach's mouth, so we all waited and watched as the coach approached the group. Often a coach would shout as he arrived for everyone to stand and begin running laps, letting us know immediately that who we were was not of first importance. The coach who came with a vision for the season, a roster in hand showing that he had an interest in who we were—maybe even with some idea of what we had done in the past and perhaps a schedule for the day and the rest of the season—would set a tone of consistency and planning. Each of these inputs provided answers for our information search and data for our questions regarding the trust relationship.

In the minds of our teammates, all of this set the tone on whether or not we should keep a wary eye or trust the coach to take good care of us. School would bring the very same watch-and-wait attitude from each of us. Every Autumn we gathered in a classroom, watching for the teacher to arrive as we talked amongst ourselves about who the teacher was, who already knew them, and what our mutual expectations might be regarding the timeliness of assignments, rewards, and consequences. In both sports and school, we learned from experience whether we could or should trust, and then decided individually if we would choose to trust that the coach or teacher would perform the same in the future.

The prescription of trust in the cognitive model works the same in our teams and groups in the workplace, as well as in our experiences with other believers and with God. Trust is a choice based on data gathered from many sources: our own experiences with previous behaviors, the current behavior, and whether or not we believe there may be a future in the relationship.[1]

So, what does this all mean when it comes to trusting God and the pain we suffer as we learn to develop a close relationship

---

[1] Adopted from Trust in Virtual Teams: Organization, Strategies, and Assurance for Successful Projects published by Routledge, a Taylor and Francis company, in 2013

with him? As we discover information about Jesus and living for him, we will choose to reciprocate with greater closeness to him and openness about ourselves. We will reveal more of our past, our shortcomings, and our flaws to God, allowing him to show us things about ourselves that we don't want to know. Our discovery of God comes by reading his Word, hearing others talk of their relationship with him, and growing in connection with other believers. Remember when Philip said to Jesus, "Lord, show us the Father and that will be enough for us (John 14:8). John recorded Jesus's response to Philip: "Anyone who has seen me has seen the Father" (John 14:9). And God went on to explain this relationship: "Truly I tell you, whatever you have done for one of the least of these brothers and sisters of mine you did for me" (Matt. 25:40).

Therefore, as we learn to understand Jesus, we grow in a more significant relationship with God. In learning to love our brothers and sisters in Christ while living in community with them, we strengthen our bond with Jesus and thus with God. In sharing with them in fellowship— getting to know each other through the acts of eating, talking, and—we learn more about ourselves and God. And we give them the opportunity to learn more about us. In so doing, we allow God into some of the barricaded rooms of our lives and memories.

I have often heard people say, "I don't need church to be a Christian." While that may be true, what people don't realize when they say this is that church is not a building, but rather the people who attend the building. When Jesus said to Peter that Hades would not overcome his church, he was not talking about a structure. Jesus was telling the disciples that the evil loosed upon the Earth would not defeat his people, the church, for he will conquer death and defend his church until he comes again in the final triumph.

"But what about you?" he asked. "Who do you say I am?"

Simon Peter answered, "You are the Messiah, the Son of the living God."

Jesus replied, "Blessed are you, Simon son of Jonah, for this was not revealed to you by flesh and blood, but by my Father in heaven. And I tell you that you are Peter, and on this rock, I will build my church, and the gates of Hades will not overcome it. I will give you the keys of the kingdom of heaven; whatever you bind on earth will be bound in heaven, and whatever you loose on earth will be loosed in heaven." Then he ordered his disciples not to tell anyone that he was the Messiah. (Matt 16:15-20)

So, when someone tells you they don't need to go to church, the building, to worship God, they are correct. Nevertheless, what they may not realize is that they do need the church, the people of God, to grow in their understanding of Jesus. God is a triune God, three in one together. In the same way God has created his people, as many bodies that come together to form one body, as a picture of God in Jesus the Christ. And as Paul wrote, each member of this body has a purpose: "For just as each of us has one body with many members, and these members do not all have the same function, so in Christ we, though many, form one body, and each member belongs to all the others" (Rom. 12:4-5). Just as the Father, Jesus his Son, and the Holy Spirit are each persons who together are one God, we each are unique and special beings in our own creation by God that come together to share our God-given gifts for the purpose of Jesus's body on Earth. Therefore, we should not fail to come together with other believers, for to not share our gifts for the betterment of other believers is to deny the very purpose for which God gave us the gifts.

As we come together with Jesus in community with his people as a part of his body on Earth, and we learn more about God through our reading and relationships with the church, many things in our past that God will come to show us will hurt. He shows us our flaws and shortcomings so that we can grow past them, shed the pain, and develop a deeper trust in him. It is only natural to not share with others those things we find to be less than desirable or acceptable in our personality and our past. We hide from the other person behind what we believe to be a more acceptable, make believe or preferred façade; a fake self. We only show the other that which we believe will reflect their expectations of us. But, as the connection grows and matures, we begin to let down the façade. We then allow our partner or our brothers and sisters, to see some of our warts and in the process we discover they still love us regardless.

Most of us are great at compartmentalizing bad memories and personal flaws. We take these compartments and barricade the way in, hoping that God will never ask to open that dusty, scarred old door. God, however, promised us that he will one day, as we walk with him and learn to trust him, stop at that door and point, asking to be permitted in so he can clear out the junk. He won't enter uninvited, but you can be sure he will ask, because he promised us when John wrote, "He cuts off every branch in me that bears no fruit, while every branch that does bear fruit he prunes so that it will be even more fruitful" (John 15:2).

It hurts when a branch is cut off. Old habits die hard and often cost us relationships that keep us apart from God. Drinking buddies, drug buddies, and gambling friends will fight to keep us dependent on those habits because it brings them comfort knowing their pain has a companion. New, healthy habits will form bringing renewed strength and new experiences as God snips off half-learnings and wholesome habits to keep them growing long and full, branching into new relationships and skills.

The old, ill-fitting friends that threaten to drag us back into bad habits will leave—along with the abuse and pain those damaging behaviors caused—as soon as they see Jesus in us. And it will hurt when they reject us and refuse to accept our renewed self, though we can be sure that God will fill that gap in our life with a healthy and loving relationship with other believers. And these believers-brothers and sisters who will come alongside you, help you to live for him.

CHAPTER 4

Living for Jesus:
The World Hates Those Who
Love the Lord

Some may bristle at the idea of viewing God as an institution due to the way in which the word implies a human origin, but we are only following God's lead in his analogy. God established several institutions that helps us understand that he is faithful and worthy of our trust. For in the beginning, when God created our world, he said, "'Let there be light,' and there was light. God saw that the light was good, and he separated the light from the darkness. God called the light 'Day,' and the darkness he called 'night'" (Gen. 1:3-5). By creating a separation of the light from the darkness, he gave a picture of a good eternity interdicted by a presence of evil for a period, declaring a beginning and ending; thus the foreshadowing of the institution of time. And his church is likened unto a bride, waiting in anticipation for the love of her life to return to her and carry her off to a life of joy and fulfillment on their wedding night. So, God also provided us a picture of the institution of God's kingdom with his people separated from the world and waiting to join their king when he triumphantly returns (Rev. 19:7). God is good and faithful. He knows that when we live for his Son Jesus, the world will hate us and it will hurt, but will lead from sorrow to everlasting joy.

Adam was created in eternity, but when Adam, having been offered an alternative, chose to disobey God, a clock started counting down to the day when we, as Adam's offspring, may return once again to eternal life. Prior to what Christianity traditionally refers to as the *fall*, mankind lived without time. Time has no use in eternity because time assumes a beginning and an end. According to *All About God*, an online blog (www.allabout-god.com), When Genesis 1:1 says, "In the beginning God created the heavens and the earth" (NIV), it does not imply that this is the beginning of time, but rather only the beginning of man's existence in the world that came to be through God's Word.

Time did not exist before the creation of man, nor did it begin with the creation of man. God created day and night knowing that we would need to be reminded every day of God's faithfulness, and provided the rising sun as an illustration of God's renewal of all things. The concept of time passing came in the curse following the fall, so we experience time as a cycle of death and renewal that God illustrates through the faithful cycle of each day. He gave us the daily cycle as a means of tracking the countdown as we wait for the time of final renewal when Jesus returns to Earth to establish his eternal kingdom.

If we think about it, we quickly realize that time has no meaning beyond the counting from an event, such as the birth of a person, or the counting toward an event, such as a child's anticipation of the end of the school year. As we live in the moment, time ceases to exist until a coming event slams back into our consciousness, and we once again feel the pressure of time. As quantum physicists recently confirmed, nothing exists until it is measured. Thus, time has a proven purpose in God's plan, pointing toward our redemption and reinstatement into paradise (MacDonald 2015). Imagine living forever in the moment, as Adam did before his fatal choice. Think of the immense weight and pressure that must have fallen upon him when he looked back at that moment and realized his mistake.

It was at that moment in eternity that time began, when Adam realized he could never go back and undo that choice. The seconds began to tick, pulling him further and further from the event. Then Adam turned toward the sound of Jesus's patient footfalls moving closer to him as the seconds ticked by, waiting for God to confront his misbehavior. And since that moment of indiscretion, we wait as time trudges forward to the final renewal.

We learn of God's faithfulness and trust by the continuity and utter lack of failure in the cycle of time. Since the creation, the sun rises and falls without hesitation, no matter the weather or events in this world. No matter what catastrophe or calamity, the cycle of days, months, years, centuries, and millennia continues unabated. All things experience time in the same way, and all things have their end. People, animals, plants, fish—even rocks and mountains rise, crumble, and fall; all things meeting their end at the precise time that God ordained. No member of God's creation can escape the countdown that began with Adam's irresponsibility.

But in our current time, God has provided us with the ability to believe he can be trusted. God is consistent and just, treating all living things the same. Through time, God also gives us a way of keeping track of significant events as necessary milestones to measure the nearing of the end of time. In the arrogance of human existence, we measure God's time forward and backward from the point of his entrance into humanity-that is Jesus's birth as a dependent, human child. However, I believe God measures our time by looking toward the chosen hour in which his Son will return as the all-powerful and ever-living King.

We must also remember that God is unaffected by the institution of time, and therefore is able to apply years equally and fairly to all things. He is unaffected because, as Einstein explained, time is relative. In this case, God stands at the beginning of time at the point of Adam's sinful decision to choose self-fulfillment, and at the end of time waiting for the appointed day of Jesus's return, riding on the clouds in triumph. Therefore, time has no influence on God's existence. God is therefore a fair and equitable arbitrator and the adjudicator of our personal allotment of time.

When nonbelievers look to God, they are looking for fairness. They ask, "How can God allow so much pain in the world?" When they ask this question, what they are really saying is, "Please, show God to me so I can believe, because this world hurts so much." As believers, we tend to fail when we answer them because we think they are asking, "Why?" But in reality, they are pleading, "Show me."

We can show them by realizing that God told us, "My sheep hear my voice, and I know them, and they follow me" (John 10:27 KJV). Show me should be an immediate clue that these nonbelievers hear his voice too. God is consistent, clear, and trustworthy to call all people to himself equally. It is up to us, those who have found their place at the table, to help those crying out for guidance—to help them see God as a trusted Father and Jesus as their trustworthy brother and King.

We can call Jesus our brother and King. Jesus stepped into history for the purpose of making us holy, making a way for us to return to sanctification. The writer of Hebrews (2:11) tells us, "The one who makes us holy and those who are made holy are of the same family. So Jesus is not ashamed to call them brothers and sisters (Hebrews 2:11)." This is because God said, "The Father has loved us so much that we are called children of God" (1 John 3:1 NCV). Therefore, we can call Jesus, our King, a brother.

Just as importantly, we are seated as an invited and treasured guest, for Ephesians (2:6) tells us that "God raised us up with Christ and seated us with him in the heavenly realms." It is essential to know this, for where we have an invitation and assigned seat, we know we are wanted members. Jesus said, "And if I go and prepare a place for you, I will come back and take you to be with me that you also may be where I am" (John 14:3). The real struggle is that many believers have not yet found their place at the table. They are still struggling with the idea that God has placed them in the heavenly realms at a time when they still live upon this earth. The drowning cannot reach out and save the person drowning next to them. So many of us sit in the pew or chair each week and sing and nod, but never really hear God's voice among the cacophony of voices screaming to be heard in our heads. We hear clearly the circus barkers of the world calling out to us, hollering the latest news, the start of the football game at noon, the demands of the job come Monday, the threats of bills coming due—on and on the voices yell, driving God's still, small voice from our ears.

But God is consistent, and we know his voice when we hear it. We all heard it once and came to his house to listen again, hoping to hear the voice that brings us hope and joy. A problem for most of us is that, when we hear God's voice, we don't recognize him. We should—we know his voice—but like Samuel, we don't realize it is our Father's voice calling to us.

The boy Samuel ministered before the Lord under Eli. In those days the word of the Lord was rare; there were not many visions.

> One night Eli, whose eyes were becoming so weak that he could barely see, was lying down in his usual place. The lamp of God had not yet gone out, and Samuel was lying down in the house of the Lord, where the ark of God was. Then the Lord called Samuel.
>
> Samuel answered, "Here I am." And he ran to Eli and said, "Here I am; you called me."
>
> But Eli said, "I did not call; go back and lie down." So, he went and lay down. (1 Sam. 3:1-5)

Samuel recognized the voice but failed to realize the voice was the Father calling out to him. We do this, all of us, missing the opportunity to participate in what God is doing around us. God is consistent and can always be trusted to be the same. God never changes. He works in us, around us, and among us, always—and always through his children, calling believers to do his work on Earth.

God was calling out to Samuel in that still, small voice. We have to learn to listen and hear when God speaks. We aren't the only ones who struggle to hear God's voice. Even the great men of the faith in the Old Testament struggled. When the world threatened to crush them, even those that walked with God had to learn to listen.

> Then He said [to Elijah], "Go out, and stand on the mountain before the Lord." And behold, the Lord passed by, and a great and strong wind tore into the mountains and broke the rocks in pieces before the Lord, but the Lord was not in the wind; and after the wind an earthquake, but the Lord was not in the earthquake; and after the earthquake a fire, but the Lord was not in the fire; and after the fire a still small voice.
>
> So, it was, when Elijah heard it, that he wrapped his face in his mantle and went out and stood in the entrance of the cave. Suddenly a voice came to him, and said, "What are you doing here, Elijah?" (1 Kings 19:11-13 NKJV)

And so it was with Eli when he realized that Samuel was hearing the voice of God, but not recognizing the still, small voice. Samuel was looking for the voice in the chaos of life rather than looking up. He couldn't hear the small voice of God above the cares of the world.

> Again, the Lord called, "Samuel!" And Samuel got up and went to Eli and said, "Here I am; you called me."
>
> "My son," Eli said, "I did not call; go back and lie down."
>
> Now Samuel did not yet know the Lord: The word of the Lord had not yet been revealed to him.
>
> A third time the Lord called, "Samuel!" And Samuel got up and went to Eli and said, "Here I am; you called me."
>
> Then Eli realized that the Lord was calling the boy. (1 Sam. 3:6-8)

When God calls us, we need to stop and listen. We must recognize his voice and say, "Here I am." It is at that point when we truly realize we have a place at the table, a home and a seat at the feet of our God and his Son Jesus. Then we truly realize our membership and we can consistently hear and recognize his voice—this is the point, beyond the cognitive discovery we discussed earlier, when we come to know our relationship with God.

We live in community with other people, and God expects us to interact and serve one another in his name. It is through the actions of others who heed God's words—his call to pray and provide, to listen and serve—that we feel God's love and care. However, even if we don't heed God's words, his will is not frustrated, for even the birds will help when no man will do so.

> Then the word of the Lord came to Elijah: "Leave here, turn eastward and hide in the Keith Ravine, east of the Jordan. You will drink from the brook, and I have directed the ravens to supply you with food there." (1 Kings 17:2-4 NKJV)

God is not frustrated. All of creation listens to God's voice and acts on his will. As Jesus descended from the Mount of Olives, riding on the back of a donkey to triumphantly enter Jerusalem, a group of Pharisees confronted Jesus, chastising him to stop the crowd of disciples from loudly praising him as their king. Jesus explained to them the power of God's will saying to the Pharisees, "I tell you that if these should keep silent, the stones would immediately cry out" (Luke 19:40 NKJV). It is when we listen that we may participate and live according to God's calling on our lives. So, Samuel listened for God's voice and recognized him.

> So Eli told Samuel, "Go and lie down, and if he calls you, say, 'Speak, Lord, for your servant is listening.'" So Samuel went and lay down in his place.
>
> The Lord came and stood there, calling as at the other times, "Samuel! Samuel!"
>
> Then Samuel said, "Speak, for your servant is listening." (1 Sam. 3:9-10)

Samuel listened when God spoke, and he grew in his relationship with God, learning to watch for God's actions that he may participate according to God's plan.

> The Lord was with Samuel as he grew up, and he let none of Samuel's words fall to the

ground. And all Israel from Dan to Beersheba recognized that Samuel was attested as a prophet of
the Lord. The Lord continued to appear at Shiloh,
and there he revealed himself to Samuel through
his word. (1 Sam. 3:19-21)

What should we do when hearing God's voice calling to us?
Answer the same as Samuel did saying, "Here I am, Lord." Then,
wait for God to give us direction. Often, God will bring someone
to the forefront of our mind, someone that we haven't thought
about for years, and ask us to pray. Our first inclination is to ask
why? But God rarely provides the explanation. He just wants us
to step out in faith and allow the Holy Spirit in us to provide the
guidance.

God does not need us in order to carry out his plans. He provides us with opportunities to participate in his plans so that we
are blessed by doing his work and so that others can see God in us
and in our lives. When we carefully listen, God will tell us what
he is doing and then we can do his will. Even Jesus said, "Very
truly I tell you, the Son can do nothing by himself; he can do only
what he sees his Father doing, because whatever the Father does
the Son also does" (John 5:19). Jesus explained to his disciples
that he did not go out seeking work to do in God's name, but
rather listened and watched to understand what the Father was
doing—then participated with the Father so that others may be
blessed as he is blessed through God's work.

I learned about 20 years ago to listen for God's still small voice
and to watch for what God is doing. By listening and watching,
I discovered that God does invite us to participate in his work,
and that through doing his will we are exceedingly blessed. One
night, a rather otherwise uneventful, peaceful night, I was listening for God after praying and worshiping in my heart. God whispered to me to pray for a coworker. It was a coworker I didn't
know but had probably spoken to at least once.

Today I cannot remember her name, but I will never forget God's request that I pray for her. It was late at night, and, being an early riser all my life, I had gone to bed early. I came awake, not sure what I was doing and thought about it for a minute. Realizing I had no idea what to pray, I prayed for guidance. God's answer was, once again, one word: "Pray." Now, I am a slow learner, so I argued, asking again for guidance, and this time I received two words. "Pray, NOW!" It seemed more like a command than a request, so even though I am a slow learner, I started praying. I prayed for protection—from what I had no idea, but it seemed urgent that I pray for protection for this person. After a while—and I have no idea today how long that was—I stopped praying and listened. It was silence once again, so I went to sleep, confused, troubled, and determined to find this person and ask them what they were doing last night.

The next morning, I went to work a little earlier than usual and looked her up in the phone directory, discovered we were on the same floor in the plant, and went to her desk. She was sitting there, gazing into her computer terminal, not moving. So, I stepped into her cubicle and introduced myself, said hello, and then asked her bluntly what was going on last night. She looked shocked. Then she asked me, "Why?"

I remember that she was very distraught that I asked her that question and she didn't answer until I explained. I told her that God woke me up and told me to pray for her. I told her of the urgency and how God insisted it was very important. "So, I prayed," I told her. I really didn't expect much of an answer, and half expected her to tell me to go away before she called security, but she didn't. She looked at me with tears in her eyes, saying, "My husband tried to kill me. He had a gun, and he was really going to kill me, then he stopped and just left."

Stunned to silence, I could only stand there, unable to respond to her tears. Then I simply said, "Well, you need to know that God loves you, and he told me to pray." We became friends after that day, and she became a believer. God used my prayers to change her life. I don't know where she is today, but I know she knows her place at God's table.

By listening and doing as our King Jesus did, we learn to mimic his behaviors and therefore learn to be good citizens of his kingdom. Jesus reminded us of this when he admonished his followers, saying, "Why do you call me, 'Lord, Lord,' and do not do what I say?" (Luke. 6:46). Jesus was asking how we can claim that he is our teacher and our King if we don't do the things he says. A king in this earthly life is considered to be a sovereign being, holding power over all aspects of his or her subject's life, including the ultimate power of life and death. Subjects to a king do what the king desires. Jesus is King of kings (1 Timothy 6:15). Therefore, if we are subjects of the King of kings, to have a seat at the table of the King, and a home that he has prepared for us in his kingdom, we are compelled to comply with what he says. To live in a kingdom is to be subject to the king.

To be subject to the king is to be under the control and jurisdiction of the king. The king is in charge and in control of our behavior and volition. To be a good and faithful subject to our king, we must be listening for his voice and watching what the king is doing that we may be able to participate in his will, giving up our own for the benefit of the king. God is consistent and dependable, never changing and always faithful to do what he says: "For I, the Lord, do not change; therefore you, O sons of Jacob, are not consumed" (Mal. 3:6).

God is always faithful to his word, and so the Apostle Paul wrote to those who were suffering persecution, "Therefore, my beloved brothers, be steadfast, immovable, always abounding in the work of the Lord, knowing that in the Lord your labor is not in vain" (1 Cor. 15:58 ESV). We can have trust in the institutions of our God for we know that as God is faithful, truthful, and equitable to all people today, he will also be the same tomorrow and always.

God is not waiting for us to be great believers, full of faith and able to make the blind see and the lame walk. Rather, he is waiting for us to listen to his voice. Too often, our desire to serve God begins with the words, "I want," rather than the words, "I will." God is faithful and consistent, never changing and always present. He is waiting for us to say, "Here I am, Lord. I am listening," so he can show the work he is doing.

I will give one more example of what God does when we simply listen. Once again, while I was sleeping, God whispered to me to pray. And, being the slow learner that I am, I woke and asked, "For what?" God told me to pray for a former coworker, someone whom I had neither seen nor talked with for over ten years. I remembered his name, and so again, I asked God to clarify. "What should I pray for?" God's answer was the same: "Just pray."

Because, if we just pray, God's Holy Spirit can intercede in our prayers and guide us according to God's will. So, I just prayed, and God gave me the words. I prayed again for protection. At some point I stopped and listened, and all was silent, so I went back to sleep. The next morning, I realized again that I had no idea how to get ahold of this person. Time had passed, and I didn't have his email, phone number, or even old shared contacts, so I started searching for him online.

After about a week, I found an email that looked like it could be his, so I sent a note explaining who I was and asking if this email belonged to him. It was, and he sent me his phone number. Not sure what to expect, I gave him a call, and like last time, I asked him what was going on that day. He told me he was on a flight from New York to Los Angeles. and ran into a terrible thunderstorm and the plane was struck by lightning. He explained that everyone on board was certain the plane was going down and they were all about to die.

Like the time before, I told him that God loves him and that God had told me to pray for his protection. He was stunned and thanked me. We talked for a few minutes, then hung up, and I never heard from him again. But he knows that God loves him. This second example shows that God will help you to participate in his work, even for someone you may not have thought about for many years.

When God works and asks you to participate in what he is doing, it may be for someone you have never met, or perhaps someone you once knew. It may be for someone you love. God's prompting is not always only in a still, small voice. Paul gave advance notice when he wrote, "And in the last days it shall be, God declares, that I will pour out my Spirit on all flesh, and your sons and your daughters shall prophesy, and your young men shall see visions, and your old men shall dream dreams" (Acts 2:17 ESV).

As a younger man, God would give me a vision of someone for whom I was to pray. I would suddenly see them before my eyes in connection with an injury or accident, and I would immediately pray. While the disaster may not have been averted, the bodily damage seen in the vision did not occur. It was always shocking and scary, but after some time I realized that God was allowing me to participate in his work.

God is consistent and fair. He provides specific gifts to those whom he chooses, but he gives all his children a gift. That way, we may participate in the body of Christ and be blessed by his work.

> There are diversities of gifts, but the same Spirit. There are differences of ministries, but the same Lord. And there are diversities of activities, but it is the same God who works all in all. But the manifestation of the Spirit is given to each one for the profit of all: for to one is given the word of wisdom through the Spirit, to another the word of knowledge through the same Spirit, to another faith by the same Spirit, to another gifts of healings by the same Spirit, to another the working of mir-

acles, to another prophecy, to another discerning of spirits, to another different kinds of tongues, to another the interpretation of tongues. But one and the same Spirit works all these things, distributing to each one individually as He wills. (1 Cor. 12:4-11 NKJV)

Institutional-Based Trust

Institutional-based trust is somewhat different, so we need to spend a minute or two to get a better understanding of trust. As we grow, we come into contact with the administration of many different institutions. To keep with the youth sports analogy as my first experience in institutional trust, one of the first things any group seeks to identify is whether everyone is truly equal in the treatment and application of policies and practices. As the team would gather, we would watch for clues as to whether the coach's kid would be treated the same as every other kid on the team. Would the coach's kid have to work as hard as the rest of us to get a starting spot in the game? The team would get an early indicator as practice began, whether or not the coach was going to play favorites based on whether his kid was automatically assigned one of the highly coveted positions on the team. If the coach's kid began practices as the starting running back, or perhaps the lead pitcher, without having to compete for the spot the same as the rest of the team, it was a clear indicator that we would have to compete to be his friend rather than the better athlete.

As kids do, the team would begin working to figure out how hard we would have to work, and what type of goofing around would be tolerated. Practices would always begin with calisthenics. As the warm-up began, team members would immediately be watching to see if the kids who slacked off during the exercise would be chastised for their weak participation. If they were ignored, then of course those with a lesser level of motivation would begin to slack off to bring their performance down to the least level of acceptable performance. All of the team members watched as the coach interacted with the players, assigned roles, and doled out chastisement and punishment. If weak performance or effort was not addressed or perhaps even rewarded—or perhaps rules were eased to aid favorite performers while at the same time strong effort was ignored—attitudes regarding fair treatment from the leaders would be adjusted.

Over time, everyone would learn what was expected of us, and what we could expect from the dad-coach. The reaction to institutional equity, or fairness, is the same in the workplace as it was in our experience on the childhood practice field. We make our decisions regarding the trustworthiness of an organization based on how we feel we are treated consistently and equally among our peers. As employees and team members, we build our sense of institutional trust based on the treatment we receive concerning the organizational policies, as well as how equitable our treatment is when compared to the treatment that others receive.[2]

"For," we can be sure, "God does not show favoritism (Romans 2:11). We are all treated the same by God who, "will repay each person according to what they have done" (Romans 2:6). And, so we can have confidence that we are treated fairly at all times knowing that, "Jesus Christ is the same yesterday and today and forever" (Heb. 13:8 ESV). Our King never changes and he expects that we, through our experience and in community with believers will, "Trust in the Lord with all your heart and lean not on your own understanding; in all your ways submit to him, and he will make your paths straight" (Proverbs 3:5). One struggle we may have is our tendency to look at fairness from our personal point of view, using our own definition of trustworthiness. We

---

[2] Adopted from Trust in Virtual Teams: Organization, Strategies, and Assurance for Successful Projects published by Routledge, a Taylor and Francis company, in 2013

weigh interactions with other people, encounters at church, and problems in life based on our personality and life experiences, before deciding that God can't be fair and equitable. However, we need to again mature our idea of fairness into an understanding of God's justice, for God is holy and just.

Merriam-Webster defines *just* as being in conformity with what is morally right, good, or righteous (June 2 2019, Definition of Just). So, when we apply this standard, we know that God is fair according to his righteousness. God gives us an example to show us that no matter how early or late in life we come to know him and his righteousness, we will be treated in the same way as those who come to know him as a child.

> "For the kingdom of heaven is like a landowner who went out early in the morning to hire workers for his vineyard. He agreed to pay them a denarius for the day and sent them into his vineyard.

> "About nine in the morning he went out and saw others standing in the marketplace doing nothing. He told them, 'You also go and work in my vineyard, and I will pay you whatever is right.' So, they went.

> "He went out again about noon and about three in the afternoon and did the same thing. About five in the afternoon he went out and found still others standing around. He asked them, 'Why have you been standing here all day long doing nothing?'

> "'Because no one has hired us,' they answered.

> "He said to them, 'You also go and work in my vineyard.'

"When evening came, the owner of the vineyard said to his foreman, 'Call the workers and pay them their wages, beginning with the last ones hired and going on to the first.'

"The workers who were hired about five in the afternoon came and each received a denarius. So, when those came who were hired first, they expected to receive more. But each one of them also received a denarius. When they received it, they began to grumble against the landowner. 'These who were hired last worked only one hour,' they said, 'and you have made them equal to us who have borne the burden of the work and the heat of the day.'

"But he answered one of them, 'I am not being unfair to you, friend. Didn't you agree to work for a denarius? Take your pay and go. I want to give the one who was hired last the same as I gave you. Don't I have the right to do what I want with my own money? Or are you envious because I am generous?'

"So, the last will be first, and the first will be last." (Matt. 20:1-16)

Is it fair, according to human reason, that someone who came to the vineyard in the last hour would be paid the same as someone who came to work in the first hour? No, but God wants us to know that it is right and just that he loves each one of us the same, no matter the time of our life in which we turn control of life over to him. He wants us to know that we can have confidence that he has a gift waiting for us so that we too may participate in his work; that a home awaits with a seat at his table for the hour that we choose his Son, Jesus. Also, that he values each one of us the same as the person that came to know him and love him as a small child.

I came to know the Lord Jesus around three o'clock in the afternoon; later in life. Rather late, but I know that God values my work for his kingdom the same as he does those who showed up in his vineyard at nine in the morning and worked all day. God is just, not fair. Human standards of fairness demand that we each be treated differently and valued by our personal standards. And I am so glad that God does not think the way we think (Isaiah, 55:8).

CHAPTER 5

There Is Joy in Trusting God

*"These things I have spoken to you, that in
Me you may have peace. In the world you will
have tribulation; but be of good cheer, I have
overcome the world."* (John 16:33 NKJV)

*And we know that all things work together for
good to those who love God, to those who are
the called according to His purpose.*
(Rom. 8:28 NKJV)

God expects that we may find great pleasure and happiness in his love and comfort, even in this world that groans and aches with suffering and pain as we take refuge in him through the helper; his Holy Spirit (Psalm 5:11; Romans 14:17). "For we are saved, not by doing good things, but by our trust in him, learning to live in God's kingdom while here in this life. For we are his workmanship, created in Christ Jesus unto good works, which God hath ordained that we should walk in them" (Eph. 2:10 KJV). The ultimate goal for the Christian life is to live for God with all of our heart, saved to do good things so that others may believe. If this were not true, would we not simply be lifted up to God upon being saved?

As we noted earlier, life in this world is filled with sorrows. Adam discovered long ago that this world is struggling with pain.

In living for God, we not only experience the struggle of living after the fall in a world permeated with illness, toils, and death, but also with the consequences of our own sin. And as we grow in our relationship with God, he will cut off the branches that do not produce good fruit. But, notice that God did not say that life will be *good* when we live for him.

Adam was born into eternity in a world without sin, pain, illness, or toiling, for suffering was not created by God. Rather our discomfort and sorrow are direct consequences of the decision made by Adam. God, in his never-ending love and long-suffering, knowing that people would choose their own path and deviate from his design, designed the consequence of sin as a means of pointing back to him.

For God promised that, although he did not create the world in pain and suffering, he did design a world in which all things will bring us home to him if only we choose to trust in him. In all things, our world offers us a choice: to do as God desires or to select an alternative—that is, our own will.

But we must ask ourselves, Why? God is not afraid of our examination, and therefore we should ask the difficult questions. Why, if God loves us, would he allow so much pain in our lives? Why would a loving God make a world where we watch our children suffer and die? Would a loving God really create such a world?

To answer this question, I want to tell you a quick story—one that depicts what is probably the most painful time in my life, and one that has taken me over thirty-five years to really grasp. It's one that I hope will help us all to know that God uses all of our pain for good when we are called according to his purpose.

The Loss of a Child

The first time I saw my daughter, she seemed to gaze so intently into my eyes. It was as if she hoped for help that I knew

I couldn't give. I looked back at her with pain and tears, praying for that same hope. We were thrown together, sharing that early December day, which still haunts my dreams and will never fade from my thoughts. Tarah was born more than two months premature in November, more than thirty-five years ago.

Will you still love me, though I could do nothing for you, but watch? I have asked myself that question over and over, dreading the day when we meet in Heaven. Will she be angry with me?

Our relationship started such innocence, such quiet. She lay there in that see-through neonatal intensive-care bassinet, unable to help herself. She looked at me, hoping for help while all around us babies struggled to survive, while desperate mothers and fathers whispered prayers of their own. There was no blood, no trauma—just a frail weakness.

Don't close your eyes. I pleaded silently, sitting beneath the hot, sterile glare of light bouncing off the gleaming white walls. I couldn't speak aloud, in order to avoid those listening nearby, but I prayed and prayed that God would give a miracle—she would suddenly be healthy and strong. Her eyes were closing. I glanced quickly about. Everybody was busy attending to the others. They were busy, but not frantic. *Please don't close your eyes.* I gave her a gentle jiggle, causing her eyes to pop back open. I knew if her eyes closed, she would be gone.

I gave her another gentle shake to keep her awake. "You're okay," I whispered gently in her ear. I lied to her. I knew she was not going to be okay. Then I hugged her close, sharing the warmth of my body to keep her comfortable. *Breathe. Keep breathing for a few more moments*, I thought, giving another soft jiggle to get her attention.

Quickly glancing over my shoulder I saw a familiar, desperate mother, tears rolling down her cheek, reaching out to touch her baby that she may never get to hold and comfort. I remember wanting so much to look strong. *You don't know me, I know, but someday you may. I hope*, I prayed. I reached out with my free hand, giving her hand a soft squeeze, and waited. It was the kind of squeeze that conveyed the message that I was here for her. And I prayed to God to stop this and heal her, thinking, *I can't do this.*

Why was God doing this?

Someone gently grasped my shoulders as I felt the warmth of their breath against my cheek. The stranger, an ICU nurse, silently watched. *I don't know you*, I thought. I tried to ignore the attention, focusing only on my daughter's eyes, watching to be sure they didn't close. Whoever was behind me gave another soft squeeze with both hands and turned away, back to the others.

Suddenly, I remembered to check on her brother, lying close by and struggling with his own problems. *He's going to be okay.* Tubes jutted *from his ribs, re-inflating his lungs.* Please, God let him be okay, I prayed quietly. "The babies will die," the doctor told me this morning when I arrived. His words echoed in my ears all day.

I believed prayers could change this situation—that my will could keep her alive if only I believed enough. Nonetheless, the weeks of no sleep and the fatigue deep down in my bones took its toll. *How long can I sit here?* I thought, as I gave another soft jiggle. *Keep your eyes open for just a little longer.* I heard another alarm sound over my shoulder and glanced up just long enough to see the white-jacketed, soft-shoed person quickly turn and hustle back to....

I didn't observe long enough to know what happened. The loud, droning tones stopped, and that was enough to bring my eyes back to her. I watched, with only a small portion of my consciousness, as a shrouded figure wheeled past, then was gone. I gave my daughter another squeeze on her tiny, frail hand. *Will you hate me if I let you sleep?*

Was that really the question? The one I wanted to ask her? The problem that kept me awake, prevented me from letting her rest? The thought slammed through my body with a chilling rush of adrenaline. She moved, only a tiny bit of a stretch. It was enough to indicate her discomfort with the tube inside her nose, supplying oxygen.

"Shh," I said softly. It seemed the only comfort I had to offer.

"There is nothing more that can be done for her," the doctor had said. "Nothing. Just be here."

Nothing. The word rattled around in my mind. *Nothing.* The echo will never stop.

Another droning tone behind me snapped my mind back to the present. And I watched. Just watched.

"It's just the oxygen levels," I heard a nurse say, adjusting the gauge with little interest.

Just?

An alarm near my side jolted me like a shock of electricity, causing me to give another jiggle. *Flatline,* my mind screamed. Another jiggle and she slowly opened her eyes. *Not yet.*

"Not now," I whispered.

"Here," the nurse said. The woman spoke very softly as she removed the oxygen tube from the tiny nose.

I knew oxygen wasn't doing her any good anyway. *I think the nurse left it on to make me feel better.*

The nurse turned to me, and with words and a nod that were exaggeratedly gentle, she said, "You can move around a little easier this way." Her hands moved with precision as she unclipped the cardio monitor. She then gestured to indicate I could move.

I turned, scanning the room with eyes that could barely focus.

Staying alive, I thought. That's the desire in every set of tiny eyes in the room.

You're supposed to fix this.

You're supposed to protect her.

You're supposed to save her.

You're supposed to make things better.

You're not supposed to watch her die.

I stretched, hoping to relieve the cramp in my lower back, careful not to stress the fragile life I held in my arms, and looked across the room. Her brother lay quietly, wrapped in his own struggle, in the transparent bassinet across the room—naked, weak, and vulnerable. The tubes in his ribs, I hate the ugly tubes that dripped blood and fluid into the plastic bag hanging from that clear, sterile bassinet.

It is warm in here.

Once again, my eyes settled on her face, burning the tiny, innocent features into my memory. The sweet, accepting eyes that believed I was there to help. I took a deep breath and stood still, holding her tiny, soft fingers in my own, determined not to jiggle her awake once again.

"Shh," I whispered. I could feel each beat of my heart painfully bumping against my chest while thoughts crashed toward the one I'd tried to avoid. That single accusing thought. *You're here to watch your child die.*

I took a deep breath and slowly let it drain from my lungs. Don't move. Her eyes fluttered, slowly drifting closed, before feebly popping open once more.

Don't move, damn it.

Her eyelids! They're closing, my mind screamed.

Don't!

Let her be.

I squeezed back that uncontrollable desire to keep her awake. *Wake her up!*

"She can't live," her doctor had told me. "Her organs are shutting down. Her body has cut off the blood supply, and she has gangrene throughout her abdomen. There is no hope. She will die, but you can make sure she knows you love her."

I held my breath and fought with every last bit of will to stand as still as possible. *Just a tiny jiggle,* I thought. *Only one more, please!* But her eyes slowly closed. My heart cried out, accusing, helpless, and angry, that I should wake her. *Just one more time, just one more look into her eyes.* Yet I stood as still as possible, not breathing.

Please! Just look at me one more time.

I looked around the room for someone, anyone, who might be able to help. A nurse suddenly appeared silently by my side, setting a stethoscope against her tiny chest, before shaking her head. The nurse stood still, without saying a word, without looking at my face. She waited patiently as I held the tiny, lifeless form in my arms.

Dear sweet little daughter. I didn't say goodbye.

I was supposed to save you.

Even today, as I write these words, tears stream down my face. The pain never goes away when we lose a child. And yet, God promises to use these things for good. I didn't understand what that meant until one day, many years later, a coworker came into my office looking distraught. For the sake of not calling my friend *him*, I'll use the name Jake.

Jake and I worked together for years in the nuclear power industry, and when I made the jump to the financial sector, he followed. We got along well and considered each other friends, but as time rolled on, that relationship seemed to shift into boss and employee. And, with many irons in the fire, Jake was wearing himself down. He was in the midst of studying to become a financial advisor, worked out of his home gym as a personal trainer, worked full time with me as an associate director, and was expecting his first child to arrive at any moment.

Some days Jake came into work pumped, excited, and burning to get to work and make his magic. On other days he dragged himself in like he was pulling an anchor, unable to make anything happen. Today, he was haggard and slumped in his chair when he sat. When I asked what was happening, he just shook his head without looking at me and said, "My baby died last night."

It was then that I knew that God could use my loss to strengthen my friend. I prayed again for strength as all of those emotions flooded back into my heart. I prayed and began to tell my story, and we grieved together. I know that God did not create that pain or death, but he was able to use the pain I suffered so many years ago to relieve a suffering father who had no idea what to do with his grief. Remember Paul's words when he said, "And we know that all things work together for good to them that love God, to them who are the called according to his purpose" (Rom. 8:28 KJV).

God is faithful and never changing. He is the same today, yesterday, and tomorrow, so we can have faith and trust in him. It does us no good to rationalize our pain and suffering, saying to anyone that, "I know it hurts, but look at our brothers and sisters in the Middle East. They are tortured and killed every day."

No one can hear that when in the midst of their own pain and take it seriously. One's own pain hurts every bit as much as anyone else's regardless of their station in life. When a parent is watching a child suffer through bullying or panicking at the thought of losing their home to foreclosure—or worse yet, grieving the loss of their own child—the pain is real. Relativity is not a balm to soothe their pain.

Our main hope is in knowing that God is faithful. Through years of suffering, he shows us that he never changes, but is always with us, ordering our days in a way to ensure our pain is used to our benefit. He is always by our side, using what is bad to fulfill our hope for what is good. So how are we called according to God's purpose?

God's Purpose

We can have joy in our sorrow and rejoice that our God is creating us anew. As we move through this painful life, we can know that God is busy conforming us to the image of his Son, Jesus. We are called to be holy, trusting in God for all things, and knowing that all things are designed to bring us home to him. And in order to fulfill his purpose, God needs to undo a lot of what happens to us in this short life. We need to see that although we may make poor decisions based on limited information, and though this cursed world is filled with sickness, sorrow, and death, he is ultimately Lord over all things and faithful to change the outcome such that we are more than conquerors over the pain (Rom. 8:38).

Joseph's brothers found his pit already dug and filled with pain as they cast him down (Gen. 37:24). In the same way as Joseph, we may feel as though someone dug a deep pit into which we were cast. The hole was dug one shovel full at a time, with each shovel ripped from the Earth beneath our feet, causing us to stumble and question God's wisdom in our lives. The first shovel was filled with the pain of humiliation before our peers when they laughed as we tried desperately to present our show-and-tell project. Or perhaps a shovel filled with dirt represents that day in second grade when our father told us he was leaving or heading off to war. Another shovel may represent never receiving an invitation to our high school's Homecoming Dance. But for many of us, the shovel represents much greater devastation in the form of verbal, physical, or sexual abuse by strangers, family members, and loved ones. For most of us, there is no limit to the number of shovels used to dig the pit into which we were cast.

In the pit, Joseph suffered thirst and hunger until he was found and taken as a slave into Egypt. While in Egypt, he had good days and bad, just like we do. Being in the pit doesn't mean every day is terrible. We have good days and bad days, and some days where we feel like we may have found our way out. Joseph was a slave, a prisoner, a good servant, and ultimately exalted as a great leader. And, in the end, he was able to say to his brothers, "As for you, you meant evil against me; but God meant it for good" (Gen. 50:20 NKJV).

Meant it for good? I know that I cannot be alone when in times of difficulty and pain I can't see anything good coming my way.

I stomp my feet and cry out, "God, it is not good with my soul," choosing to throw his own words back at him in my frustration. But, in the end, after all the tears, shouts, stomps, stomachaches, sweating, and shudders of fear, anger, and frustration, I can say God is good.

For I have held my child in my arms and watched as she closed her tiny, innocent eyes for the last time. And when the pain receded, and with her face indelibly etched into my memory, I learned of God's goodness when he turned the pain into a blessing for a suffering brother.

On a steamy, soggy, thunderous summer day, I saw our town destroyed by an F5 tornado and every last, little belonging wiped from our lives. The smell, sights, and fears of that day will never be lost. However, I also saw God wipe away debts along with the belongings, allowing us to own a new home at a time when our double income shrunk to only one. God turned devastation into a blessing in the blink of an eye.

God carried us through cancer, heart disease, heart attack, and not months, but years of unemployment; never once has our suffering gone without God's blessing and protection. On and on your list may go, but God is always faithful and trustworthy to give us peace and good cheer in tribulation—making all things right for those who return his love and are called according to his purpose. Matthew described for us a question from the Pharisees when they asked Jesus which was the greatest commandment? Jesus replied that "Love the Lord your God with all your heart and with all your soul and with all your mind" is the greatest of all the commandments (Matt. 22:37).

How Do We Love God?

How do we love God? We listen carefully to what God says, hang on his every word, care for his body, love his Son. Or otherwise stated, we live in a relationship with him. When God speaks, as we talked about earlier, we listen. We scour through the passages of conversations transcribed for us in his holy book, the Bible. Most importantly, we love and care for his body and his Son.

God tells us to never forsake gathering together with his faithful so that we may continuously give to one another strong encouragement (Heb. 10:25). As we have discussed throughout this text, none of us will make it through this life of sorrow and pain without the support and encouragement of our brothers and sisters. For years, I believed that I was upholding my end of the bargain. I attended church faithfully, rarely missing my Sunday morning obligation to attend to the sermon, listening to the preacher and singing in the crowd of believers. I remained a face in the crowd for almost thirty years, happy to arrive late and say hello when the preacher prompted us to greet someone we didn't know. This, by the way, was easy because I was careful not to get to know anyone.

I did do my part and volunteered as an usher, doing my duty one Sunday a month, and on holidays when the need arose. Nonetheless, I was also careful to not know anyone beyond a courtesy "Good morning" and a firm handshake. Then, one Sunday, I must have been tired and slow, failing to duck out quickly when the final song finished. My wife and I always sat in the back, near the exit, ready to make a quick escape. But on that Sunday, one of the ushers blocked the path. I obviously allowed him to get a little too close to me. He greeted me with a firm handshake and a smile, asking if I was interested in attending home fellowship with him. He too, never got beyond the kind handshake during the preacher's pre-sermon prompt.

A lot of strange, unconnected questions bounced around in my head as I rapidly contemplated his invitation. How can we be fully used and available to God's purpose if we are not plugged in as a part of the body of Christ? Can a hand be a useful hand if there is no arm connecting it to the rest of a body? And can the rest of the body be whole and fully effective without the hand? The apostle Paul tells us, "You are the body of Christ. Each one of you is a part of it" (1 Cor. 12:27 NIRV).

I think the answer is obvious. We must be connected to one another to fully love ourselves, our brothers and sisters, and God. We must also be connected to our brothers and sisters to be fully used and useful to God—and to better learn to trust in God for all things.

> There is one body, but it has many parts. But all its many parts make up one body. It is the same with Christ. We were all baptized by one Holy Spirit. And so we are formed into one body. It didn't matter whether we were Jews or Gentiles, slaves or free people. We were all given the same Spirit to drink. So the body is not made up of just one part. It has many parts.
>
> Suppose the foot says, "I am not a hand. So I don't belong to the body." By saying this, it cannot stop being part of the body. And suppose the ear says, "I am not an eye. So I don't belong to the body." By saying this, it cannot stop being part of the body. If the whole body were an eye, how could it hear? If the whole body were an ear, how could it smell? God has placed each part in the body just as he wanted it to be. If all the parts were the same, how could there be a body? As it is, there are many parts. But there is only one body.
>
> The eye can't say to the hand, "I don't need you!" The head can't say to the feet, "I don't need you!" In fact, it is just the opposite. The parts of the body that seem to be weaker are the ones we

can't do without. The parts that we think are less important we treat with special honor. The private parts aren't shown. But they are treated with special care. The parts that can be shown don't need special care. But God has put together all the parts of the body. And he has given more honor to the parts that didn't have any. In that way, the parts of the body will not take sides. All of them will take care of one another. If one part suffers, every part suffers with it. If one part is honored, every part shares in its joy. (1 Cor. 12:12-26 NIRV)

I often said hello and talked with the usher who invited me, he was a nice guy and we got along, so I agreed to meet him at a local home-fellowship gathering the following Friday evening. It was there, in fellowship with other believers on a regular basis, that I came to fully understand my relationship with Jesus, and my growth in trust and love rapidly grew. In this connection with other believers, our prayers are more fruitful as we come together and agree in prayer (Mathew 18:19-20). We raise our voices and hearts together in one prayer, enjoying communion with the body of Christ.

But how does this help us love Christ? It is through giving and sharing with brothers and sisters that we express our love for God. Matthew reminds us of Jesus's words: "Truly I tell you, whatever you did for one of the least of these brothers and sisters of mine, you did for me" (Matt. 25:40). Believe me, there is ample opportunity to share within our home fellowship. This is because as the body of Christ grows in number, it also grows in strength and intimacy, allowing everyone to share both their gifts and sorrows. Among a group of believers we will always find someone who's child is struggling in school, or a daughter dating a boy who is a bad influence, and someone struggling with drugs, alcohol, or pornography. Someone's relative has cancer or friend is ill and dying. Stepping in and offering to cut their grass so they can focus on their need is a simple act of love. As we learn to share with one another, we also learn to share with others, therefore sharing in God's purpose as one body.

Whom Does God Call to Him?

For those who hold to the greatest of the commandments of God, there is a promise that all things work together for our good. But what about the second qualifier? What does it mean to be *called according to his purpose*? To answer this question, we must begin with understanding whom God calls. Matthew tells us that God calls many people to him; according to John, no one can come to know and trust Jesus unless they are called to this knowledge by God the Father (Matt. 24:12; John 6:44).

In his letter to Timothy, Paul reminds us that God did not choose anyone due to the great things they did in their life, nor due to their wonderful intellect, their kind heart, or their hard work. God calls each one of us to him so that we may fulfill his purposes in our lives and the lives of others (2 Tim.1:9). Paul also wants us to understand that God calls us so that he may give us his gift of eternal life. This is not because we have somehow earned this gift, but because, in his love for us, he has worked through the millennia to return us to the state of goodness in which humankind was created.

The biggest question any one of us can ask is not whom God calls, or even if God is calling me, but rather, what do I do when God calls? Recall the passage earlier in this text when we discussed Samuel? God called to Samuel, but only when Samuel responded did God guide him in his response.

Sometimes all we have is a feeling. Not everyone will hear, or perhaps recognize, God's voice when he calls. And, yes, I said the F-word, *feeling*. I don't like this word, but it is indeed accurate in this case. God gave us examples of not recognizing his voice, and instead feeling his presence in our heart. In one example, Cleopas and another disciple were walking on the road to Emmaus and talking about Jesus's miracles and teachings, and about his capture and crucifixion (Luke 24:13-14). At one point, Jesus joins them as they discussed the events, but they did not recognize him (Luke 24:15). After Jesus explained to them the fulfillment of the prophesies through his ministry and death, "Their eyes were opened and they recognized him" (Luke 24:31). "They asked each other, 'Were not our hearts burning within us while he talked with us on the road and opened the Scriptures to us" (Luke 24:34)?

Fleeting feelings are dangerous, however it is even more dangerous to ignore the feeling when God calls. Job described the feeling as though his heart trembled or pounded in his chest at the sound of God speaking (Job 37:1). Others expressed the feeling as a burning sensation, saying, "My heart grew hot within me" (Ps. 39:3).

I had the feeling as well, and I ignored it for years. Whenever a believer dared to share the Word of God with me, my heart would burn as if someone was tugging at the very muscle itself. Others describe the feeling as yearning, but whatever you call it, don't ignore it, for we are all called by God. The calling is irrevocable, Paul said when writing to the people of God's church in Rome (Rom. 11:29). But God's voice, the tugging at your heart, can be dulled by your determination to ignore him.

What Is God's Joy?

But in all things, God says, he gives us joy. I did not find joy in my sorrow until I stopped ignoring his call and came to know Jesus as my Savior. Still, his joy remained limited until my connection with Jesus blossomed into a trusted relationship. Yet I still struggle to explain the joy we have in God when someone, whether they be a believer, seeker, or unbeliever, asks me, "What in the world do you mean by God's joy?" But when I listened to the pastor speak, I understood. Isn't God awesome in the way he continues to unfold his message, given to us in measures by which we come to know him better?

The pastor's message began very unassumingly, for the day was December 23, just two days before Christmas. Therefore, I expected a message about the baby Jesus and the traditional, *get yourself ready for Christ's coming* supplication we have all grown up hearing. There was so much on my mind as the holiday rolled in, and the stressors of out of state visitors and final holiday preparation merged with the daily grind of work, family, bills, and stresses of holiday expectations, that I almost didn't listen. My wife and I live-streamed the message on our computer as we went through our morning.

But the message took a strange twist into the story of the apostle Paul and Silas as they traveled through Philippi, hounded by a little girl who was possessed by an evil spirit. The girl was driven by the spirit to follow them through the city so that the demon could steal their message. You see, even the devil and his demons know God's message.

Satan taught his evil demons to twist God's words with half-truths to make their message sound appealing as Satan did when he quoted Psalm 91:11-12.

He took Jesus to the highest point on the top of the God's temple in Jerusalem attempted to entice Jesus to test God's promise to protect Jesus saying, "Throw yourself down (Matthew 4:5). Of course, Jesus resisted the need to prove God's words true, chastising Satan. The point is, Satan understands God and knows God's words, for Satan was once a holy angel created in eternity—the same as man was created into eternity before the fall.

For several days, the demon-possessed child followed Paul and Silas throughout Philippi yelling, "These men are servants of the Most High God, who are telling you the way to be saved" (Acts 16:17). Imagine how irritating it would be to have someone following you around work or school and every time you tried to tell someone about Jesus, the annoying kid stood behind you shouting, "Hey everybody, Tom knows the way to be saved by God."

You cringe and watch as people turn and point, and quickly walk away jeering and mocking. Over the top of the demon's cackle, you hear shouts among sneering giggles as someone hollers, "Jesus loves you," causing the crowd to howl with more laughter. And before you can begin your message, the opportunity is lost. Eventually, even for a humble, gentle believer, the pressure is too great, and you snap—taking hold of the power God gave you for your own benefit. Then you shout in anger, "In the name of Jesus Christ I command you to come out of her!" (Acts 16:18).

These powerful words set in motion a series of events that even God's apostle would not have anticipated. This child was a slave of men, and one by which her owners earned a very comfortable living. Imagine an army of demons working in concert, scheming to deceive an entire city into believing a child could foretell the future. Acts 16 tells us, "When her owners realized that their hope of making money was gone, they seized Paul and Silas and dragged them into the marketplace to face the authorities. They brought them before the magistrates and said, 'These men are Jews, and are throwing our city into an uproar by advocating customs unlawful for us Romans to accept or practice'" (Acts 16:19-20).

When we read God's Word, it is hard to see the people behind the familiar sentences. They were severely beaten, caned in the public square, and thrown in prison. A punishment of caning was carried out by whipping a person across the shoulders and back, the back of the legs, palms of the hand, and often on the soles of the feet, with a thin, hard rod that would cut the skin and muscles, leaving behind long open wounds and deep bruising.

The apostle and his companion were handed over to the jailer for causing a disruption in the city. Keep in mind, Paul was not approached by the local police who stopped and chastised them for public disturbance. They were arrested by an occupying army determined to keep the land under Roman control, preventing any possible uprising or displays of discontent. Roman leaders allowed the local government to remain intact and the people to continue to govern in their traditional ways as long as the region remained peaceful. So, when a city was riled up the way the people of Philippi were, the noise and passion were quashed without mercy.

Paul and Silas were beaten, jailed in the innermost cells, and placed under the direct responsibility of the head jailer. They were likely shoved against the wet, rough wall, chained naked and cold, every nerve end burning, twisting their bodies, desperately trying to escape the pain as their open wounds continued to bleed. Nausea weakened them as agony throbbed across their bodies. They whispered their prayers, not wanting even their breath to cause them to move and aggravate the gouges on their torso.

And God wrapped his arms around them like a father rescuing his children from their pain. Do you remember being a suffering child wracked by the pain of influenza, or perhaps after the crisp burn of road-rash after crashing your new bicycle? I can remember racing down a hill on my new bike, still feeling invincible and unbreakable. The bike felt solid and unshakable, so I was trying out new tricks I'd seen on our old black and white tube television. I stood on one pedal at the side of the bike and hopped back in the seat. No problem. I jumped up and down on the pedals, feeling unstoppable.

I was putting on a show and decided to cross my legs over the center bar, and after that, stand on the seat. It all looked so easy on TV, and I was on a roll, so I went for it, crossed my legs, and *wham*! The bike folded under me like the last domino in the row, falling splat to the ground.

I skipped like a rock whipped down the road, ricocheted off the curb back into the street, and finally rolled to a stop. There was asphalt stuck in wounds on my knees, elbows, hands. After a while, I pulled myself to my feet and looked around, relieved my audience was only make-believe while simultaneously searching for help. Wrapped in sharp, stinging pain with every step, I hobbled to our door thinking what a blessing it was that I crashed right in front of my house.

As my mom enveloped me in her arms, my pain immediately gave way to a feeling of safety. Mom absorbed my suffering, protecting me from any further harm. She washed my wounds, spread a salve to prevent further damage from infection, and wrapped me in her arms again so I knew I was safe. She took my pain on herself with empathy and love, closing the door in order to prevent any disruption of the calm, peace-filled time of healing. I felt joy in her ability to create a place of covering love and to take on my suffering as her own.

This is the joy that God provides in times of suffering and pain. He covers us in his love and takes the weight and pain of our afflictions upon himself as he wraps his protective arms around us. Paul and Silas felt that joy as they sat in the basement of the jail with God's arms wrapped around them. Joy is not dependent on a feeling of happiness or a lack of pain. Rather, it is the knowledge that God is in control and can be trusted to take our suffering upon himself, carrying our burdens in times of trouble. Joy comes from knowing that God is good all the time, and at all times, God is good. Joy does not remove our pain or suffering, but instead gives us the comfort of knowing that God is in control and will use our painful experiences for good.

When my child died, there was no joy, for I was not a believer. There was only suffering and pain. This was the sorrow of loss that someone feels when they don't fully understand the Word of God, unable to see God's goodness and comfort in the time of bereavement. Like the apostle Paul counseled the Thessalonians,

I was filled with the same sorrow as the apostle Paul cautioned against to the people of Thessalonica, the deep and helpless pain of losing a loved one that is felt by someone who has no hope (1 Thess. 4:13). But, on the day that my friend came into work grieving the loss of his child, I was comforted by Jesus and filled with his joy as we both mourned and cried together. God is good and enabled me to share his love with this suffering father.

So as God fills us with joy in times of misfortune, hardship, and loss, he also rejoices with us as we comfort those around us and show them his joy. And, as we pray with joy according to God's will and in Jesus's name, he rewards our prayers and gives us those things for which we pray (1 John 5:14). And we can know God's will when we do as Jesus did—by watching what God is doing and then praying that God will allow us to participate. Remember, even Jesus said he can do nothing except with the help of the Father.

"Very truly I tell you," Jesus said, "the Son can do nothing by himself; he can do only what he sees his Father doing, because whatever the Father does the Son also does" (John 5:19). The apostle Paul and Silas watched the jailer as they sang praises to Jesus for giving them the comfort and joy they required in a terrible situation. Paul and Silas heard the prisoners around them as they listened, and perhaps even attempted to join their singing while wrapped in their own suffering. And Paul and Silas prayed according to God's will for the hearts of those listening to their voices.

God's answer was likely much greater than their prayers, for God often gives us both that for which we pray and that for which we have a need. God knows our prayers, but we also take comfort in knowing that God knows our needs much better than we do.

Earlier, I mentioned a massive tornado. Well, at the time my wife and I were suffering financially due to her loss of a good job. We wondered how we would pay our bills but chose to continue to trust in God as we paid our tithe and held our breath, hoping my income would cover our bills each month. We prayed for relief but never expected the answer would include the total destruction of everything we owned. The tornado crashed through the town, causing death and destruction to everything in its path.

As the dust settled, we grieved over the loss of our home and furnishings, our cars, and all the memorabilia from our wedding and our childhoods. After the grief subsided at the loss of life suffered by our neighbors, we came to realize that we also lost all of our debts and the decay of the older home we owned. We received so much more than we lost. After the pain subsided, we knew God's blessing in our shiny new home and furnishings. Above all else, we could now afford to live on one income.

Just as we did not expect God's blessing to come in the form of a massive, destructive storm, Paul and Silas did not expect God's answer to come in the form of an earthquake.

> About midnight Paul and Silas were praying and singing hymns to God, and the other prisoners were listening to them. Suddenly there was such a violent earthquake that the foundations of the prison were shaken. At once all the prison doors flew open, and everyone's chains came loose. The jailer woke up, and when he saw the prison doors open, he drew his sword and was about to kill himself because he thought the prisoners had escaped. But Paul shouted, "Don't harm yourself! We are all here!" (Acts 16:25-28)

Paul and Silas then had an opportunity to share God's love with the jailer and the other prisoners. I am confident the apostle did not expect God to shake the foundations of the prison or to break them free of their bonds. In the process, they converted the hearts of the jailer and other prisoners when they prayed for comfort, praising God. Yet this is how our God, the almighty Father, works—in a whisper.

CHAPTER 6

Trust and Follow:
For These Pains Are Pains of New Birth

Then Jesus said to his disciples, "Whoever wants to be my disciple must deny themselves and take up their cross and follow me."
(Matt. 16:24)

And he said to all, "If anyone would come after me, let him deny himself and take up his cross daily and follow me." (Luke 9:23 ESV)

Do Not Be Fooled

We need to understand at this point, how Satan works to twist God's words to cause us to wander from the truth. At times, Satan and his demons are so efficient in their work that it appears as if he is in all places at all times and knows the future. Not at all. Satan's demons are finite, just as you and I are. However, unlike you and I, they are a part of a large army moving in the shadows and manipulating people in such as a way as to appear as if they are foretelling the future. When it works out, they look like they can see things before they happen, when in fact they are only running ahead and influencing the gullible, greedy, and self-serving into behaving badly. Then, they take a bow and cause the unbeliever to turn to them for advice and guidance rather than forming a reliance on and relationship with Jesus.

Paul and Silas understood when they cast the demon out of the fortune telling slave girl of Philippi (Acts 16:17) that anything miraculous that does not point to Jesus as the source is not of God, but of an evil origin. I encountered this firsthand as a seeker, when trying to find my way toward Jesus. To give a one-sentence history, my wife and I were in our twenties, both recently divorced, and living together. Yet we realized we needed to do something with this "Jesus" thing.

We decided to visit some churches and asked friends to make recommendations. We attended a new church each week and sometimes more than one on Sunday, trying to find someone who could connect us with Jesus. One Friday evening, we visited the church of a friend. The group met in an old house. It seemed as though the light from outside could shine through the siding of this place as we sat in old, scarred pews. There were fewer than a dozen people scattered throughout the tiny main room, seated alone.

The service began with a few traditional hymns, including one of my favorites: "The Old Wooden Cross." When the voices faded, the person behind the lectern asked for song requests from those seated in the tiny crowd, then suddenly pointed behind my wife. She mentioned someone by name who had somehow requested the very song to which my wife opened in the hymnal. I turned around with a smile, thinking I would thank the patron behind me, only to find we were the last ones in the back. There was no one there. "Amazing Grace" it was.

We looked at each other with a weird grimace and began to sing. After a short and simple presentation that seemed very traditional on the surface, the speaker said that she had a *message* for someone in the crowd and turned to me. She told me, "I see you driving. It's a beautiful day. You're passing green, lush, well-manicured lawns, bordering a wide, slow curve. As you make the final turn, there is your children's school bus. It was hit in the back by a small red car and burst into flames. But, don't worry, your kids are okay."

I smiled and nodded thinking, *Yeah, right.*

During the drive home, we talked about the service and pretty much put it out of our minds. Then, a few weeks later, I decided to take a different route to pick up the kids from school. My children from a previous marriage always rode the school bus to my sister's home and would stay there until I could pick them up after work. It was a warm and sunny spring day. I drove through the neighborhood, around beautiful, lush, well-groomed lawns on a lazy curve, and as I made the final turn, I saw my children's school bus. It was engulfed in flames and had a small red car smashed beneath the rear emergency door.

I braked hard to a stop, threw open the car door and burst forth, hitting the ground running. I ran toward the crowd of people standing around, some of them pointing toward the red car sticking out from under the bus. As I approached, someone grabbed my arm, stopping me from going forward as they said, "Don't worry, your kids are okay." And at that moment, the preacher's words crashed back into my consciousness.

That freaked me out. In my mind I could see the preacher's face before me, looking at me, smiling and saying, "I told you so." At that moment, I knew this could not be from God, because it was the Preacher who took the glory, not Jesus. Needless to say, we did not return to that church.

Better to Trust in God Than Man (Psalm 118:8)

Now that we understand what it means to trust, and we have taken a moment to assess our own level of trust when it comes to our Lord and Savior, Jesus the Christ, how do we follow Jesus?

According to the MacMillan dictionary, to follow in someone's footsteps is to "do the same work or achieve the same success as someone else before you" (MacMillan 2018). That definition begs the question, "What would Jesus do?" This question became popular in the 1990s with the acronym and slogan "WWJD." When we remember that God is always the same and never changes, we understand the real question to be, "How do I act in a way that is consistent with Jesus?" Jesus told us what to do when he told his disciples to deny themselves.

One of my most fervent prayers is for God to take away my own desires and to replace those desires with his own. That prayer is one that I struggle with on a daily basis. Most of us want to be liked and looked up to by those around us, especially if you have ever held a position of strength and influence at work or in your community.

Giving up that power and glory is not an easy thing. Society in the USA teaches us that the smart and beautiful people, those whom we should seek to emulate, grace the theater screens and come into our homes through the ever-present television. The message is that they alone have the intelligence and have the answers to all of the world's problems; they alone have the message that leads to health, satisfaction, wealth, and power.

We need to resist the message to follow the celebrity and pray daily, "God, please take away my own desires and replace them with your own." Matthew 16:24, "Whoever wants to be my disciple must deny themselves and take up their cross and follow me," does not mean that we should pretend to be pious or to act as though we don't have any needs. Rather, we should recognize that we may have a desire to be seen doing great things. The verse means we need to acknowledge that we need to deny our own wishes, and that we should not be ashamed to share our story.

As a young person first entering the corporate world, I took a job as an industrial mechanic at a major electric power producer. I began my work life in training. They started with the basics, telling us what tools were used to do which tasks. One thing that always stuck with me was a question designed to help align our goals with the training. The instructor asked us, "What are your goals for this job?" Everyone came up with some simple version of wishing to give their families a better life.

But, when he came around to me, I said I intended to make enough money to someday drive a Mercedes to work. The instructor laughed, telling me to go home and rethink my goals. I never did take too kindly to being laughed at, so I set off on a quest to make that kind of money—and eventually made it, working as a director in a major financial firm. But when I had the chance to purchase the car, God stopped me, reminding me that just because I wanted it, that didn't make it okay. He helped me set aside that desire at a time when the needs around me were greater than my need to make that instructor stop laughing.

God wants us to align our desires with his desires. Remember, God said that if we pray according to his will, he hears us (1 John 5:14). So, what is God's will? I believe that God's will is that everyone comes to know that he gave his Son to us as the perfect sacrifice so that we could someday come home and live with him in eternity. Therefore, all of our actions should point people to Jesus and his suffering for forgiveness of our sins.

But, what of the other half Matthew 16:24 that referred to the taking up of our cross? Jesus said that not only do we need to deny ourselves, but that we must also take up our cross. That one line was always baffling to me. How do we take up our cross?

The cross was a Roman tool of torture, but also a device of shame. When someone was sentenced to hang on a cross, they were stripped naked, scourged, and nailed to the crossbeam, spread across the wood for everyone to see their shame. Jesus wants us to set aside our pride, sin, and fear. He wants us to open ourselves up and allow him inside the darkest places of our lives and memories so that he can use our weaknesses for the will of the Father.

Jesus is asking us to realize that our sins do not disqualify us from doing God's work. He wants us to understand that the sins that fill us with shame also allow God to work in us to guide other people to trust in him. Allowing God to dig deep into the corners of our memories and pull out that shame for the world to see is what creates the power in our testimony to those addicted to pornography, drugs, alcohol, sex, power, or any other worldly pursuit that afflicts our community.

When we accept God's offer and pick up our shame to follow Jesus is when the real, powerful journey begins. However, it takes trust to allow God into the dark and dusty crevices in which we hide our shame. That is why God told us to be like little children, trusting in him the way the babies trust their caregivers. A small child is not afraid to come running down the hallway, still wet from jumping naked from the bathtub—too excited to stop, dry off, and put on their clothes. They know they are loved and accepted just the way they are. That child knows you will wrap them in your arms and love them, wet and naked.

God wants us to trust in him in the same way a small child trusts their mother and father. In reality, the problems of a child are the same problems we have as an adult. We were simply ignorant of the problem because those issues were handled for us. As a child, our home very likely was still mortgaged and the vehicle in which we rode was probably under a lease or purchased with a loan. The food on our plate was still purchased from a store, and the electricity was still expensive. We just didn't worry about these things because our parents or caregivers worried for us. God wants us to have that same faith in him today, as we did in our parents when we were young.

So, let go of your own desires and pick yourself up, allowing God to see and use your shame for his purposes. As God told the apostle Paul when he prayed for God to heal him, "My power is made perfect in weakness" (2 Cor. 12:9).

Jesus told his disciples that if they were to have faith, even faith the size of the tiniest seed, they could tell mountains to get up and move, and the mountain will do as they ask (Matt. 17:20). I have seen people healed by prayer, storms whipped up that clear the foundation and give a new start, and the fury of a storm stopped by the prayers of children.

I remember one day in later summer when the children were still very young and out for a short day-trip with their mom. The day was hot, and the air felt like a wet blanket when I stepped out of the cool, conditioned air. The wind was whipped into a frenzy by the rising heat and the storm rumbled in, throwing large hail and sheets of water against the house. I remember praying, thanking the Lord for keeping my babies safe and for showing my children how much he loved them.

At the end of the day, my wife and children came into the house. Their faces were shining with brilliant smiles and they told a triumphant story of God's love and protection. The children all talked at once, their voices mingling in agreement. They told me how the storm terrified them, how they were crying and screaming as the wind crashed against the car—and torrents of rain and hail battered the vehicle.

My wife, Nancy, told them to pray, for she too was scared. As they prayed together, a hole in the storm opened above them. And the storm, for them, ceased. Although all around them the violence raged on, the sunny day followed them home. Our children never forgot that experience, and since that day, they have prayed with confidence for friends, family, and their own needs.

"I can do all this through him who gives me strength," Paul tells us in his letter to the church in Philippi (Phil. 4:13). Jesus tells us to follow him, or in other words, to do as he does. Now, many people try to tell us that God no longer provides miracles in our time. But I know better, for we can see evidence of God's miracles when we look. People are still healed and lives are still made new when we trust in his Son, Jesus.

To follow someone is to do the things they do. So, we, as Jesus said, are expected to watch as we wander through this world— seeing what God is doing, and then praying. We are expected to act to take part in what God does. For, like Jesus explained to his disciples, he can do nothing apart from what the Father is doing (John 5:19). Jesus told his disciples that with only a tiny bit of faith, they could command demons in his name, we too can heal the sick, and if necessary command the very rocks of the Earth in his name (Matt. 17:20).

And, while we do have suffering in this life, our pains are birth pains as we are reborn into a new Earth under God. For God's Word says:

> When a woman is giving birth, she has sorrow because her hour has come, but when she has delivered the baby, she no longer remembers the anguish, for joy that a human being has been born into the world. So also you have sorrow now, but I will see you again, and your hearts will rejoice, and no one will take your joy from you. (John 16:21-22 ESV)

> Who shall separate us from the love of Christ? Shall tribulation, or distress, or persecution, or famine, or nakedness, or peril, or sword? As it is written: "For Your sake we are killed all day long; We are accounted as sheep for the slaughter." Yet in all these things we are more than conquerors through Him who loved us. For I am persuaded

that neither death nor life, nor angels nor princi-
palities nor powers, nor things present nor things
to come, nor height nor depth, nor any other created thing, shall be able to separate us from the
love of God which is in Christ Jesus our Lord.
(Rom. 8:35-39, NKJV)

"If the world hates you," Jesus said to his disciples, "keep in
mind it hated me first" (John 15:18). Hate is a powerful emotion.
It drives people to do terrible things. We can see this in the lives
of believers living in the Middle East as they struggle to survive
amongst people who hate Jesus and his followers with all of their
being.

Hear, O Israel: The Lord our God is one Lord: And
thou shalt love the Lord thy God with all thine
heart, and with all thy soul, and with all thy might.
(Deut. 6:4 KJV)

These things I have spoken to you, that in Me you
may have peace. In the world you will have tribulation; but be of good cheer, I have overcome the
world. (John 16:33 NKJV)

So, if you now understand that Jesus is God and that God is
trustworthy, please pray with me.

Dear God, I know I'm a sinner, and I ask for your
forgiveness. I believe Jesus Christ is Your Son. I
believe that He died for my sin and that you raised
Him to life. I want to trust Him as my Savior and
follow Him as Lord, from this day forward. Guide
my life and help me to do your will. I pray this in
the name of Jesus. Amen. (Graham 2018)

References

Barrett, L.F. 2017. "This is how your brain constructs emotions." *Popular Science*. www.popsci.com

Bastable, S. B. 2003. *Nurse as Educator: Principles of Teaching and Learning for Nursing Practice*. Jones & Bartlett Learning.

Bibles for America. "What is the heart in the bible?" *Bibles for America* (blog). September 7, 2015. http://blog.biblesforamerica.org/what-is-the-heart-in-the-bible/.

Blaine, J. 2018. "7 biggest misfits of the Bible: The stories in the Bible tell of black sheep, oddballs and rebels just like me and you." (blog). www.beliefnet.com

Boteach, S. 2011. "No holds barred: Can love exist without hate?" *The Jerusalem Post*. www.jpost.com.

Brown, S. L. 2012. "Fantasy and its effect on your reality: Emotional suffering is created in the moment we don't accept what is." *Psychology Today*. www.psychologytoday.com.

Bryner, J. 2007. "Study: Your personality can change (and probably should)." *LiveScience*. www.livescience.com.

Bugeja, M. 2017. "Algorithms, evil & augmented reality: The desensitization of Facebook users." *Interpersonal Divide in the Age of the Machine*. www.interpersonal-divide.org.

Cleese, S. 2017. "Love without hate." *Gender Theory*. www.medium.com.

Connor, S. 2008. "Scientists prove it really is a thin line between love and hate." *Independent*. www.independent.co.uk.

Gettel, J.J. 2003. *God's Love, Human Freedom, and Christian Faith*. Chalice Press: St. Louis, MO.

Graham, B. 2018. "Begin your journey to peace." *Peace with God* (blog). www.peacewithgod.net.

Griswold, E. 2015. "Is this the end of Christianity in the Middle East?" *New York Times*. www.nytimes.com.

Gutierrez, E. 2013. "Attachment: Building trust in your infant." *MSU Extension*. www.canr.msu.edu.

Hamada, O. (2016 November). 3 reasons sin and holiness can't coexist. [blog]. www.omarhamada.com

Humberman, B. 2016. "Growth and development, ages 13 to 17: What parents need to know." *Advocates for Youth*. www.advocatesforyouth.org.

Jarvenpaa, S. L., & Leidner, D. E. 1998. "Communication and trust in global virtual teams." *Journal of Computer Mediated Communication*, 3 (4), 1–36.

Lewis, T. 2013. "New theory explains why amputees feel phantom limb pain." *Live Science*. www.livescience.com.

Live Science Staff. 2010. Personality set for life by 1st grade, study suggests. *Livescience*. www.livescience.com

MacDonald, F. 2015. "Reality doesn't exist until we measure it, quantum experiment confirms." *Science Alert*. www.sciencealert.com.

MacMillan Dictionary, s.v. "Follow in someone's footsteps," accessed December 2, 2018, www.macmillandictionary.com.

Mayo Clinic. 2018 "Phantom pain." *Mayo Clinic*. October, 2018. www.mayoclinic.org.

Merriam-Webster. May 24, 2019. *Definition of Abide*. https://www.merriam-webster.com/dictionary/abide

Merriam-Webster. May 24, 2019. *Definition of Sacrifice*. https://www.merriam-webster.com/dictionary/sacrifice

Merriam-Webster. June 2, 2019. *Definition of Just*. https://www.merriam-webster.com/dictionary/just

Mizrachi, N., Drori, I. & Anspach, R.R. 2007. Repertoires of trust: The practice of trust in multinational organization amid political conflict. *American Sociological Review*. 72, 143-165. Retrieved from http://www.asanet.org

Piper, J. 1985. "Called according to His purpose." *Desiring God*. www.desiringgod.org.

Praver, F. C. 2009. "Love without hate ain't no love at all." *Psychology Today*. www.psychologytoday.com.

Riley, L. 2017. "Too damaged to love again." *Christian Broadcasting* Network (blog). September 18, 2017. http://www1.cbn.com/marriage/too-damaged-to-love-again.

Sanders, L. 2014. "Love requires trust." *Spirit and Truth Blog* (blog). May 5, 2014. http://spiritandtruthblog.com/love-requires-trust/.

Sarker, S. J. Valacich, & S. Sarker. "Virtual team trust: Instrument development and validation in an IS educational environment." *Information Resources Management Journal* (IRMJ) 16, no. 2 (2003): 35-55.

Schatzline, P. 2015. "Unqualified: The messiah's misfits." *Charisma Magazine*. www.charismamag.com.

Schnider, A. 2008. *The Confabulating Mind: How the Brain Creates Reality*. Oxford University Press, Inc.: New York, NY.

Sherwood, H. 2018. "Christians in Egypt face unprecedented persecution, report says." *The Guardian*. www.theguardian.com.

Smith, K. 2018. "Love is a choice more than a feeling." *PsychCentral*. www.psychcentral.com.

Stewart, D. 2018. "How do we understand the serpent in the garden of Eden?" *Blue Letter Bible* (blog). October 20, 2018. www.blueletterbible.org.

Tristam, P. 2017. "Christians of the Middle-East: Country-by-country facts." *Thoughtco*. May 22, 2017. https://www.thought-co.com/christians-of-the-middle-east-2353327.

Uebersax, J. "Scripture's Heart: An Empirical Study of the Word 'Heart' in the Bible" (blog), October 12, 2012, http://www.john-uebersax.com/plato/heart1.htm.

Wise, T. 2013. *Trust in Virtual Teams: Organization, Strategy, and Assurance for Successful Projects*. Routledge; New York, NY

Index

Printed in the United States
By Bookmasters